From the Other Side of the Bed

A <u>Woman</u> looks at life in the family business

From the Other Side of the Bed

a Woman looks at life in the family business

by **Katy Danco**

with an introduction by **Léon A. Danco, Ph.D.**

THE CENTER FOR FAMILY BUSINESS

university press, inc.

Post Office Box 24268
Cleveland, Ohio 44124

Library of Congress Cataloging in Publication Data

Danco, Katy, 1929-
  From the other side of the bed.

  1. Executives' wives. 2. Family corporations.
I. Title.
HQ759.6.D36   306.8'7   81-13032
ISBN 0-9603614-2-1   AACR2

First Printing: September 1981

Printed in USA

*to those who make
my life complete:*

Katy
Tyler
Ty
Suzanne
Barry
Mema
Great

...and, especially,

Léon

Table of Contents

introduction by
Léon A. Danco, Ph.D.

The greatest difference between a family-owned business and any other form of business is that there is a *family* (and, eventually, *several* families) involved *together* in that business. Failure to recognize the implications of this simple fact ruins (sooner or later) more outwardly "successful" privately owned businesses in this country than taxes, inflation, bureaucratic governments, and cutthroat competitors all added together.

Over the years that I've had the privilege of getting closely involved with families in business, including my own, these people have taught me everything I know about the challenges, the frustrations, the heartbreaks and the joys of business ownership.

But I am only a man. I can only know, see, and hear (and, with luck, understand) from the perspective of a *male* —a business *man*, a founder. For many years, I didn't even recognize this fact. It was just there. I looked at business ownership in much the same way as the clients and seminar participants I knew did. It was a *man's* activity.

I didn't even allow women to attend our seminars in the early days. As far as I was concerned, there could be only two outcomes to such a thing, and I said so. If the women were good looking, they'd be distracting. If they weren't, they'd be discouraging. Sure, I said that for effect and it got laughs, but underneath, it represented something of what I then believed.

But somewhere, somehow, I found something was missing. I found I was only hearing half a story—and not necessarily the more important or better half. Today, as far as I'm concerned, no seminar is complete, no speech is fully worthwhile, no client consultation is valid if the *women* involved are ignored or just kept as pets. Their influence has had a great and beneficial effect on the beliefs and understanding I have today.

It's easy to think of women as "incidental" to the privately held business. Even the IRS seems to share this attitude. (Consider their attitude against the deductibility of a wife's expenses!) Whatever changes women may be experiencing as a group, business is still a man's world. In spite of all the wishful thinking indulged in by certain pressure groups, men today still run most of our businesses. Men still found most new businesses. Most successors to business owners are still men. It remains easy to relegate women to the dubious status of powers "behind" the throne.

It's easy, but it is dead wrong. The influence, the power, and the impact—for good or for ill—of the women in families owning businesses is immense. The numbers alone should have told us this years ago.

Consider: There are, in round numbers, some 10-12 million privately held businesses in this country, (only one-tenth of which are incorporated). So there must be something more than 10-12 million wives, widows, ex-wives, and future wives of business owners. To include among them a couple hundred thousand women actively in charge of these businesses wouldn't be unreasonable. We could also estimate that there must be anywhere from 10 to 20 million business owners' daughters, and the same number of daughters-in-law of business owners.

If only one woman in 10 (and our research shows the proportion to be closer to one in five) is active in her business, this means there are probably a total of three to five million women working with their menfolk in their family business, and of these, an untold number are actively planning on being in charge in the future.

As if this enormously involved audience were not large enough, let us also remember the wives, daughters, daughters-in-law, sisters, ex-wives, and widows of the founders and partners who have come before us—and who still may be around! Is it any wonder that recognizing a family tree, and the varying perspectives of the women in it, is probably as important to a good understanding of our family businesses as our organization charts and our financial statements?

My wife Katy is in so much better a position to write a book like this than I or any other man could ever be. Together, she and I have met thousands of women involved in family businesses, but only a woman is able to see through a woman's eyes and feel what a woman feels. These women have been able to explain things to each other and to Katy that they've probably never been able to explain to the men in their lives.

As a reader, you are about to take part in rare and vital conversations, about subjects, and a group of people, never before addressed, much less understood. I have spoken and written many times before about how the business owner is lonely, tired, harassed, confused, misunderstood, running out of time, and seemingly unaware of where to go for help, but because I am not a woman, I have all but ignored the fears and hopes, the joys and frustrations of that person inhabiting "the other side of the bed."

Thanks to the cooperation, trust, and candor of all the women who provided the flesh, blood, and emotion for this book, Katy and I now hope these women will no longer be ignored.

This is not only a book for women. I might go so far as to suggest that this book is probably more for men than it is for women. At least women have some feeling for what they've contributed to the survival of their family business. They understand where they hurt, if not why. They can see the places where they could help, if only we men would let them.

It is time that we men understood, too.

Let's hope we learn to listen and understand. Let's hope we learn to express ourselves. Let this be a first step in establishing the open communication that is so important among *all* the members of our family.

Léon A. Danco, Ph.D.

Prologue

We come in many different forms, we women in family businesses.

We can be mothers, daughters, daughters-in-law, sisters, wives, and widows. We can be full working partners, potential successors, part-time officers, fictional directors, or not involved at all. Whatever our role, we are *not* second class citizens who exist just to be bought off with offerings, placated with winter tans and fashion shows, or amused with Polynesian cooking classes at conventions.

We are not the women *behind* the men. We are the women *with* the men. In most cases, this means we're the women behind the business, and I've learned that the woman behind a family business is the major strength or weakness of that business.

A successful family business can reach its full potential only as far as the women in that family are willing to participate in the dream. The future depends upon their willingness to understand and accept the demands their venture together puts on everybody's time, talent, and energy.

The support of the business owner's wife is essential, of course. The Boss has some very great burdens. Like any other leader, he's mostly alone. It's hard for him to find someone to talk to, someone to give him a a reasoned "no" or "let's wait" when it's necessary, someone who can provide a supportive "yes" that has no strings attached.

But just as the business owner is not the only man in the business family, his wife is not the only woman. It may seem at times in this book that I am talking only to the business owner's wife, but this is not true. I am speaking as well to daughters, daughters-in-law, sisters, cousins, ex-wives, second wives, partners' wives, and widows. Their support is just as essential. Their questions and concerns are just as important. What is said here applies equally—if in different ways and measures—to all.

QUESTIONS WE MUST ANSWER

As women in family businesses, we face some important and difficult questions. To list a few:

1) *How do we help our husbands if they won't talk to us?*

2) *How do we become good listeners without surrendering our own right to be heard?*

3) *How do we define our relationship to the business so that we feel fulfilled, so that we can feel that we own that business together with our husbands?*

4) *How do we understand and divide our roles, so that some women can bring their work or their leadership, while others can contribute support—all tempered and amplified by love?*

Without answers to these and many other questions, a family in business just won't succeed.

Take, for example, the question of getting our husbands to talk. Our husbands need equals, peers to talk with, somebody with whom they can identify, both emotionally and intellectually. But they usually can't find such people in the business, so their wives, most often, are the only people they can talk to.

The problem, of course, is that our husbands are doers, not discussers. This is why we have to become self-educated, active, not passive, listeners. Our problems are just as important as theirs, and getting everybody's problems discussed whenever and wherever possible can be a key to our security and happiness together.

There are many unique ways to solve this problem. I know of one woman whose husband comes home with a "news headline" about the day's events. I know of another wife who makes two martinis and climbs in the tub with her husband—and I dare anyone to keep quiet under those conditions.

This book is not only about these questions, it's also about ways other women have found to solve them.

UNDERSTANDING "THEIR" PROBLEMS

To be helpful to our spouses, we have to have some idea what kinds of concerns we should watch for. Here are a few:

1) *They become too attached to their work* . For The Boss, building a business is a little like having a baby. Raising and nurturing that business requires great intellectual skill and emotional energy, but it also provides deep satisfaction. It's a bit of immortality, and this is why he can't or won't give it up or pass it on without a struggle.

When Dad's successor tries to take over that creative act, The Boss sees not a transfer of power so much as a form of kidnapping. He often forgets he doesn't have an endless management contract with the Lord, so it becomes our role to remind him that he must plan for succession. It becomes our job to help him work toward his new career, retirement, to make sure his abilities won't be dumped on the scrap heap.

We must also help our children and their spouses to understand why they can represent a threat to their father, and, finally, we have to understand all this ourselves, so that our conflicts and needs don't add to an already difficult problem.

2) *They are overworked and frustrated* . The owner-manager is a—if not *the*—major asset of the company. He almost naturally works harder than everybody else—and probably does the job better than anybody else. His successors are under pressure to do more than their father, yet they are kept from doing so by circumstances seemingly beyond their control.

Somehow *we* have to understand why and how our husbands tend to take so much onto their shoulders. We have to recognize why and when they take the usual way out—escaping by smashing golf balls out of sight, or drinking too much, or simply crawling into a shell.

Our role is to help them find relaxation, not an escape. We have to teach them how to slow down, how to enjoy what they have, especially their families. But first we have to encourage them to share their concerns. They are not workaholics. They are "workalovics."

3) *They are alone* . Many men feel that calling on others for help is being indecisive or an admission of weakness. Our husbands love us and want to maintain our respect, so some feel they can't tell us when they hurt. Other husbands feel the business and all the problems are just too complex for anyone else to understand, that their business and their pains are "different."

Many times, too, they feel they have learned not to mention problems to us because we only get upset and make matters worse. Our role here, as wives, is first to set up circumstances where our husbands can feel that we want to hear their concerns and, second, that we see doubt as a sign of their strength, not weakness.

4) *Their priorities are constantly confused* . In any issue involving both family and business, deciding which comes first is not simple. Each is so important to the other that we have to find ways to sort priorities, so that neither the business nor the family is neglected.

We are used to this kind of balancing act. It's a lot like that day we took our first born to his new school. It was such a big step for the little guy, because he was about to spread his wings. But when the time came, he started to weep and tearfully begged us not to leave, to take him home. As our hearts broke, we untangled ourselves and pushed back. The parental instinct made us want to hold and comfort him, but we also knew it was time for him to begin to live his own life, to become independent.

The business needs this kind of care and courage, too.

5) *They are growing older*. This may be more of an immediate problem for The Boss, but his successors fight it, too. Our aging males become more and more concerned with the time that is passing, the things that aren't being done, and the dire possibilities implicit in the future.

The aging male equates his passing the business on to his successor to "giving up." He thinks he has nothing to live for. His successors think nothing can happen until Dad leaves—and time's a'wasting. This is where we can help.

The Boss has to understand that letting go of the business is not equivalent to entering a nursing home. Successors have to understand that patience is not the same as wasting their lives waiting. And we have to help them both understand each other.

6) *They are unreviewed.* The business owner tries to build a world around himself where nobody can question his policies and his decisions. He thinks he's comfortable that way. Naturally, his successors are unreviewed, too. Often it seems to them that nothing they do, or can do, will make any difference to Dad or their place in the company.

This situation leads to The Boss asking us for agreement and acceptance, while the successors ask for support and encouragement. The problem, of course, is neither one of them is too crazy about asking for—or accepting—advice. Especially not from a woman...

7) *They don't know how to explain.* There's no question that the business is complex, but if our males can understand it, so can we. The problem is, if they remain silent in their shells for too many years, they'll prove themself right—there's no way they can educate us all at once.

If we seem a little dumb, it's because The Boss made us so by assuming we want only to be kept as pets.

WE HAVE CONCERNS, TOO

These are but some of the places where we can help the men in our lives adjust to and thrive in the world they inhabit. But if this was all we had to be concerned with, this would be a much shorter book with a much different title. The reason this book is not titled something like "Helping Men Succeed in Family Business" is my belief that we women face just as many problems and challenges as they do.

This book is about life in the family business as *women* live that life. It is about the many wives, sisters, daughters, daughters-in-law, and widows I have met. It is about how they have lived, faced, and coped with the challenges thrown in their paths.

The best of these women believe they must work with the man they have. Through this faith and loyalty, they have managed to help their husbands, their brothers, and their fathers-in-law to better enjoy the fruits of their considerable labor. But at the same time, they've managed to take control of their own lives, to become vibrant, growing persons on their own.

It is to women in family businesses—and to the men who have shared their dreams with us—that I dedicate this book. I dedicate it to them both out of respect for their courage, and out of gratitude for their openness, honesty, and support.

Without their help and understanding, the unsung heroines of the family business would remain unsung.

KLD

The Wife
of an
American
Hero

Chapter 1

Surviving Life with "The Boss"

I recently received a letter from a young woman, 29, who's the wife of a new entrepreneur. He started his business three years ago and is still struggling to make it work. Her job is staying home, caring for their two youngsters, three and five.

In her letter she told me she was beginning to wonder if she could stick it out. "Is it all worth it?" she asked.

After three years, the 12-14 hour days, the lack of available funds, and the uncertainties of the future were beginning to wear her down.

Her task at the moment is at least as difficult as her husband's. As much as she loves her children, they are not enough. She lacks adult companionship. Her husband comes home after working 14 hours of every 24, so tired that he falls right into bed.

Even when he *is* awake, he's been wrestling with his problems so hard and so long that the last thing he wants to talk about when he gets home is those same problems—if he wants to talk at all.

Whether or not it's done consciously by him, she's being shut out. No matter how explainable or even understandable her situation is, it still doesn't ease her burden.

She feels apprehensive because every cent they have is being plowed back into the business. When friends discuss the delicious veal they had at their favorite restaurant, what she remembers is the cold meatloaf eaten *alone* at the kitchen counter.

Her children don't understand what their father is doing. They only know he's never around. So she constantly finds herself in the position of trying to explain, without letting her own frustrations come out, what Daddy is doing and why they don't see very much of him.

IT'S WORTH THE STRUGGLE

It's easy to see how she can question the price they're paying, but there are some good reasons why she should stick it out.

Once the business is established, soundly run and growing, it can provide the owner-manager and his family with one of the best of all possible worlds. Here's why:

* *A successful business allows room for freedom.* Business ownership is lonely in the beginning because there's nobody around to help. But with success, that loneliness translates into the opportunity to plan our lives—as well as anyone

can these days—to permit the dreams to come true.

* *A successful business allows the time to enjoy that freedom.* That is, of course, assuming it is well-run. A major time investment is necessary up front, but it builds time dividends for the future. Eventually, others can do the building.

* *A successful business generates the funds needed to put our freedom and individual philosophies into some effective form.*

Business ownership can be worth its sacrifices because it allows our families greater freedom of choice in determining how and where they will live, and how they will pursue their happiness and satisfaction. Money does make a difference.

But life in the family business is no bed of roses, particularly for the women involved. The men have their work. They have the everyday challenges and victories to balance their frustrations and fears. Not so their spouses.

(*It may seem that I am ignoring the problem of the woman owner-manager, whose spouse is a man, but really I'm not. A spouse is a spouse, male or female. Many of the concerns and problems are the same. If I concentrate on the wife of the business owner it is because she is by far the more common possessor of this problem.*)

If the family business is under-studied and misunderstood in our society, it's fairly certain that the roles of women and wives of men working in these businesses are downright *ignored*. Yet the woman in that family company can be as much the cause of its success or failure as Dad and the successors themselves— sometimes she's even *more* important.

AS WOMEN SEE IT

To help all of us toward a better understanding of the important role of women in family business, a number of years ago research was started on their challenges and problems. The comments below are only a sample of the many thoughts and feelings shared with me by many hundreds of women, but they present a fascinating glimpse into many important relationships.

There aren't many answers, of course, but bringing up some of the questions goes a long way toward gaining some understanding of the kinds of problems we women face, day to day, in the family business:

The Working Partner

Nearly 20 percent of the women we've worked with were actively involved in the business. For them, living with the boss is both a problem and a fascination.

As a young woman told me: "It's really tough when you get mad as hell at your boss and then have to go home and sleep with him."

The working spouse of a business owner faces a kind of dilemma, described by one woman to me as a problem figuring out how to shift roles from Girl Friday to Loving Wife in a matter of minutes.

"There's nothing easy about working all day alongside your husband," she said, "and then coming home to wash clothes, fix dinner and get the kids to bed. After all that, you're supposed to fix *him* a drink because *he* had a hard day!"

But working with "Dad" isn't all negative:

"The big plus to working together is that you can share the same dreams, hopes and aspirations. There's a sense of togetherness. You aren't merely happy for him when things are going great and sad for him when things are going badly. You are happy and sad *with* him. You feel part of something that is very special to him and that's what life is all about, belonging.

"You feel that you are contributing. You feel that you are not merely reaping the harvest—you're helping to plant and cultivate the crop."

Love and marriage can take on whole new dimensions for the working partner. Consider how tough it is to keep the stars shining in your eyes when you are sitting across the table from that man who yelled at you in the office a few hours earlier.

"I probably threaten to quit at least once a week," the wife of a distributor told me. "I think I'll give it all up, never go to the office again, train someone else. I'll just retire, play tennis, do volunteer work, and join clubs like the other gals—but then I ask myself if I really want to detach myself from my husband's life, his dreams, and his love.

"The answer, I know, is obvious."

It's obvious to her and, I'm sure, to many of us.

The Struggle

The wife's role in a family business in many cases is very great in the beginning—her help is inexpensive (some would say "cheap"), she's committed, and she loves the boss. This can flower into a beautiful working relationship, or it can cause some problems.

I remember one case of a couple who worked very hard together in the beginning, but gradually the husband became consumed with the business. He divided himself in two—giving the most that he had to his business. When she eventually left her job to have their children, she became more and more a part of that other, neglected side.

But working together isn't the only answer:

"I wish I had quit working and helping Cliff at the office sooner. It was necessary for me to help him for a few years when there was no other way and it meant our survival. But I got hooked and stayed on too long.

"We got into real competition with each other. I realize now that I invaded my husband's 'space.'"

The struggle itself can bring a great satisfaction and joy, a benefit explained very well by a woman who no longer worked with her husband, but kept in close touch with the business:

"I love it," she told me. "The joys are many and varied. We are always meeting new and interesting people who teach us new things. The business always leads us to new horizons and our perspectives on life are constantly being redefined."

The "Role" of the Boss's Wife

Reactions to the responsibility of being the "Boss's Wife" are as individual as the women involved. A common feeling, though, seems to be one of frustration—wanting to help, but sometimes not knowing how.

"The major difficulty," a wise woman once said to me, "is finding a way to help him cope without actually *advising* him."

There's also a sense of sadness experienced by women who have to watch their husbands put in long hours of hard work, who see them worry and feel there's no way they can be of any substantial help in solving the business problems.

Then, too, the Boss's wife often finds herself in a lot of conflict about who she is and who she is supposed to be. In the words of a woman who felt this problem deeply: "It's very taxing and can become very unreal, because I'm not the person the employees expect me to be."

Another woman said, "We live in a small town. How do I react to the wives of our employees? If I'm friendly, I'm patronizng. If I keep to myself, I'm stuck up. If I have nice things, they envy me. If I don't flaunt my privileges, they think I'm hiding something. You can't win!

"If I work," she said, "I'm meddling. If I work elsewhere, I have no interest. If I don't work at all, I'm a parasite...and the same things are said about my kids."

Also, there are always those long, lonely nights when we wonder and worry about his health and the fact that he drives himself too hard, but there are also the great times, the good things:

"Being involved with the business gives me the chance to help and to really understand what my husband is doing—his victories and, more important, his problems. Working and struggling together is a binding cement in any relationship, including marriage."

The Listener

What's it like, filling this position called the "sounding board"? I'll let the women who live it answer:

*"My husband dosn't really *tell* me things," one woman said. "It's more like he's bouncing ideas off me to see how they sound coming back to him."

*"I think the best way to describe it is that he doesn't ask questions so much as he makes statements. He knows that anything he tells me will be held in confidence and that I'm not a threat to him. That's not really true about anybody he works with."

*"I'm really convinced that if my husband didn't have an understanding wife, he'd be the loneliest man in the world."

But sounding boards have feelings, too:

The Worrier

"I've told my husband that I have an active imagination— very active. If he doesn't tell me what's going on in the business, well then I'm going to imagine what's going on and blow it all out of proportion. When things are looking dark, I'd rather know the worst than know nothing."

We heard some of these imaginary problems from the victims who thought them up in their loneliness: working late translated into an "affair"; not being at his office became an "accident"; spending money on his wife was changed to "why is he doing it?"; and not spending money on the family meant that bankruptcy was imminent.

Believe me, what this woman said about the creativity of a woman's imagination is absolutely true. We heard this expressed many times, and in many ways.

The Workaholic's Therapist

Someone has to try to keep The Boss afloat despite all of the pressure he's under. Someone has to keep him from working himself to death:

"In the early days of the business, my husband was under all sorts of pressure. He tended to take his anger and frustration out on me and the children. It would seem there was really no way out of the situation other than to quit, and there was no way we could do that.

"I think if a man has the guts to start a business, he just has to be a workaholic. It's in his blood and we're not going to change him. The solution, I think, is to join him, plunge into it together in whatever ways we can."

We have to remember that workaholics have to be treated with some pressure, like alcoholics. There was a woman who got her husband away from the business by telling him that she was going someplace for a weekend off, with or without him.

"*Most* of the time," she said, "he comes."

The Mediator

Then, of course, there's the problem of keeping a kind of emotional balance within a family made up of very strong egos. Many women have said they always seem to be the person *between* Dad and the children. According to Dad, kids today don't have the same drive to work that their fathers have, and that causes all kinds of friction that requires some mediation from Mom.

"It almost seems to be a role that women *have* to take," a mother of five told me, "because men just don't seem to be geared to it. I mean, people are really more important than things. Men tend to think with their heads, but I believe women tend to think with their whole beings."

The Retirement Counsellor

Finally, many women build lives of their own to fill the long hours their husbands are gone, only to discover Dad's plans for "retirement" are going to tear those lives out from under them.

"My husband's goals for retirement might be quite a bit different from what I have in mind," a friend explained to me. "I was in the business with him for a while, but really it was mostly 17 years with him on the road and me at home. I developed a life of my own.

"Now I'm scared that when he retires he's going to want to take all my time, that he'll be annoyed if he doesn't have my whole attention. But, you know, if I have him around all day all of a sudden, I don't know what I'm going to do because I don't know what *he's* going to do."

This woman knew that her husband's dreams of playing golf as often as he wished, or puttering in his garden to his heart's content, was going to become a bore very quickly. And once they paled as reasons to get up in the morning, he was going to look for something else—probably something supplied by her.

"I worry that he's going to want me to change my life when he retires," a woman who was very active in volunteer activities said. "In the first place, I've taken on some responsibilities in this community and I don't want to retire from that. He may want to start traveling or move south. That would cut me off from everything I am doing."

These are just some of the major questions and conflicts women face in living with The Boss. They've only begun to be explored.

ᘓᘓᘓᘓᘓᘓᘓᘓᘓᘓᘓ

Chapter 2

Success Isn't Always Easy

Having been a business owner's wife for the past 30 years, and having known and worked with many hundreds of wives of owner-managers over that time, I've learned that there are a numb er of hard questions the business wife would like to ask the "president" in her life. Since many women seem to put off asking these questions, I thought I'd do the asking for them, in the hope that some of them might get answered, somehow, someday.

> *Dear Mr. President:*
>
> *I have a few questions I've always wanted to ask, but didn't because I either didn't want to bother you, or I was afraid you wouldn't answer. I should have asked them long ago:*

* *Why is it that when you have a business "concern" you wait until it is a full blown "problem" before you share it with me? If we discussed the "concern," we might be able to solve it before it becomes a "problem."*
* *Why is it that our children have to be given all the hard, dirty jobs just because their Dad is The Boss?*
* *Why is it that when I make a business suggestion, you smile and ignore it, then in two weeks you come up with the same idea and think it's great?*
* *Why is it that you think that my day as a homemaker consists only of TV, baby sitting, and coffee with the girls?*
* *Why is it that our son-in-law, who has already held a responsible job outside our business, has to start at the bottom and be treated as an outsider?*
* *Why is it you don't tell me when money is tight? You'd be surprised how adaptable I can be if you'd just be honest with me.*
* *Why can't I find a way to tell you that I'm not comfortable with your lawyer and that if something happens to you I want a lawyer I can relate to?*
* *Why is it I can be elected to set up and administer the budget for the Art Museum, yet you feel my ideas on finance aren't worth your time?*
* *Why do you tell me "Don't worry; if something happens to me, John the Banker will take good care of you?" I'd rather you'd share your plans with me.*
* *Why is it that I work full time for you without a salary?*
* *Why can't you discuss with me the business problems you're having with our children, instead of closing me out and trying to solve them yourself?*

* Why don't you take the time to share your dream with our daughter-in-law, who just can't understand why you work her husband so hard and long?

* And when are you going to plan a long weekend with no business—just us?

I have more, but these might be good for starters...

> Love,
> Your Willing Partner,
> Katy

Most of these questions are problems of misunderstanding, caused by a lack of communication. The things we need to understand the most are the least likely to be explained properly. In fact, I think it's unusual if they're explained at all.

It's not hard to see how this can happen. Have you ever been confused when someone repeated a pet story of yours and you could hardly recognize it? Remember how you wondered how something so simple could get so distorted?

Explaining is a lot like that. Anyone who wants to get others to understand what we know, anyone who wants to teach (and a business owner, more than most, needs to be a teacher) must always remember that no matter how much we know what we have said, we just can't be sure of what was heard.

My "letter" to The Boss really asks a lot of questions about things I'm sure he feels he's already explained. The problem, of course, is that, somehow, we never hear the answers.

HEARING IS NOT UNDERSTANDING

I had an occasion not long ago to visit a friend who had suffered a stroke and couldn't speak without considerable effort. Each morning while I visited her in the hospital, a bouncy nurse would come in and, in a voice three to four times as loud as necessary, she would bellow at my friend: "Good morning—can you tell me today's date?"

A few minutes later the speech therapist arrived and said (as though she were speaking to a child): "Today we talk about you!" With a big smile, she asked a lot of questions. "What is your name?" "Is this your hand?" "Where is your foot?"

Poor Ruth, no wonder she looked angry and frustrated.

"We know you can understand us, Ruth," I said to her as soon as those "professionals" left. "It's not what you think. This 'pre-kindergarten' test she was giving you was to see what the stroke damage was. Sometimes, people understand, but can't say certain words."

She gave me a big smile and managed a "thanks."

These professionals weren't ridiculing Ruth. They were just so familiar with what they were doing that they forgot to explain to Ruth the purpose of their work. They thought they were helping, but they were making her feel worse.

The key to successful teaching—successful communication in general—is to do everything possible to make sure the intended message is, in fact, what has been *heard.*

My friend Ruth understood the words that nurse was saying. Her hearing wasn't impaired, so she didn't have to shout. But while she thought she was being friendly, Ruth *heard* her testing her to see whether or not she was a "vegetable."

The therapist was diagnosing which areas of Ruth's brain were affected by the stroke—a necessary preliminary to helping her. But Ruth *heard* her talking to an idiot. "I'm a human being," she probably wanted to shout. "I can think and I can feel."

But Ruth can't shout. She can hardly even talk. What she needs most at this point in her life, while she struggles with this frustrating illness, is some sign that others understand her.

This was obvious to me as an outsider. I heard what Ruth heard, but the people doing the speaking only heard what they *said.*

Every business owner should ask himself whether what seems so commonplace to him is being understood by his listener. Too often, he'll discover that it's not. Instead, he'll realize that when he's not understood, he starts raising his voice, assuming if he raises his voice it will be easier for the "nitwit" to understand him.

It is one thing to explain, but it's another thing to be understood. The only way I know of to be sure that our audience knows what we've said is to take the effort to know them, to find out what they heard, and to bring that in line with what we meant them to hear.

In communication, nothing is "given." Too often, people assume that others understand, or that they've "heard," and even that they agree with things they know nothing about.

LONELINESS IS NOT KNOWING

The example of a woman I met last year comes to mind.

I first met Cora at one of our seminars. We spent a lot of time with her and her husband, Tony, during the program, and promised to keep in touch afterwards. Well, as so frequently happens, we lost touch after a while.

Three years later, totally unexpectedly, Cora called me. She was in town visiting her sister and offered to take me out to lunch.

"You probably won't be surprised, Katy," she was saying, "but Tony hasn't taken all of the advice he got at the seminar. In a lot of ways, he's proceeding along the same lines he always has. For instance, he still hasn't done anything about getting that board of outside directors. He still controls everything and makes all the decisions about business, investments and things like that. He just doesn't want anyone to tell him how to run the business."

"Maybe, Cora," I said, "but I seem to remember he listened very well to us that night in Hawaii."

"Well, he did at the time, I suppose. And he *is* more willing to listen now," she answered. "More so, even, as he gets older. He's just not used to doing it yet. We've had several long discussions, and he tried to listen to what I had to say."

"But you seem worried, Cora," I said.

"I am. Recently Tony made some changes which really got me upset. He talked them over with me first, but I told him I didn't like them and why. He ignored me. Lo and behold, a few weeks later he came home from a company meeting, announcing he'd made his key man president and he was now chairman of the board. Skip, our son, was made vice president of sales. At first I couldn't understand why he did all that."

"Now you do?"

"Tony is a heart patient, which you probably know..."

"Hadn't he had one attack when we first met?" I asked.

"That's right. Well, I'm beginning to think a great many of his decisions have been made with an increasing sense of urgency. I can see a lot of problems developing."

"What kinds of problems?" I asked.

"Well, shortly after Skip came to work for Tony, they started having 'planning meetings' at the office or Skip's apartment, after hours, so they could plan to do the things they wanted to do. Tony's idea was to begin planning with Skip to keep him informed and involved. He felt he'd be able to see how Skip would work out by doing this together. It seemed like a good idea, so I never expected it would develop into a barrier between me and my son. I know Tony never expected it.

"But later, when Skip would be at the house and business matters were discussed, and I attempted to interject opinions and suggestions or asked what they were talking about, they said 'Oh, you wouldn't understand, Mom, you don't know anything about running the business.'

"Well, this really hurt, since my whole life has been affected by the business. My reply was that if I didn't know about the business, it was because I wasn't being told anymore what was going on. That seemed to make it worse. Since then, Skip has tried to avoid discussing business matters in front of me."

I nodded in understanding. Cora's problem was not unusual.

"What's happening is an alienation of my son and me. Tony didn't see this until we sat down and had a long talk and I explained to him what I felt was happening. On top of that, if Skip has problems at the office with his Dad, he is reluctant to come home to visit or have dinner or anything, because he doesn't want to be around Tony during the times they are having problems.

"And when they *do* get along, they hold meetings and I don't hear about what transpired. I'm feeling more and more left out. They don't realize that after Tony dies, most of my livelihood will depend on the success or failure of the way Skip handles the business. I feel I should at least be aware of what Tony is trying to teach Skip, and what the long range plans are.

"I know that Tony is making an effort to explain things more often now, and at his most recent meeting with Skip he told him my feelings and urged him to keep in better contact as a member of the family. Skip may become president of the company, but he will always be my son. I don't want anything to destroy that relationship.

"Katy," she said, "the last thing I want is part of the operation of the business. I even prefer to have the estate Tony leaves to me to be separate from the business, because I don't want Skip to feel obligated to look after his Mom. I want to be independent and able to do what I want to with my money."

"How's Tony's health now, Cora?" I asked.

"Oh, I'm upset about that, too. His life now is being spent preparing the way for Skip to move up as smoothly as possible and as quickly as possible. When I see Tony planning more and more for Skip's future and less for our life together after his retirement, I get depressed and just a little bit jealous.

"I think that if remaining active and at the head of the business for years longer to prepare the way for Skip shortens Tony's lifespan, I'll be very unhappy and I'll feel cheated... cheated because I had always thought that the last years of our life rightfully belonged to each other."

The waitress brought more coffee as we sat silently for a few moments. I could see in Cora's eyes how deep her concern really was.

"*All* the years together belong to you both," I said. "Tony's trying hard to plan for the future, Cora, to do what's best for both you and Skip; and it's up to you to do what you can to make sure *today* isn't wasted."

She looked up, quickly.

"But how do I do that?"

Her question was hard to answer. She was doing pretty well already, making sure Tony and Skip understood her concerns, but Tony was going to be a tough problem.

Most likely, Cora won't be able to change him, but she did decide to try for compromises. She was going to ask him to give her gifts such as weekends, or leaving the office paperwork at the office. She was going to get him to start spending time away from the business now, asking Skip to help with that, because she knew it would be good for him to get his hands on the controls and fly solo for awhile. She was going to ask him to bring her into his plans whenever they would affect her, and to do that *before* he brought them up with Skip.

Cora agreed to try all of this, although she was very doubtful. She's quite a woman, though, and if anyone can keep things together, she can.

Her problem is one that's faced by many women. Again and again over the years, women like Cora have told me how hard it is to find someone to share their thoughts, particularly someone who understands the problems and can offer support.

In some cases, this loneliness has resulted in bitterness, but I believe that these women don't have to give up. There are solutions. Business ownership can be a great life—as long as those of us on the female side of the "balance sheet" are willing to take the initiative in keeping the lines of communication open...and as long as we are willing to share and learn from each other.

CXXXXXXXXXXXO

Chapter 3

The Business Is a Problem Child

No matter how we got involved in our family business—through marriage, through birth, through inheritance, or through our own efforts, it quickly becomes an intimate part of our lives.

Like a marriage, a business is always there. If we're going to be happy and fulfilled, we're going to have to learn all of its quirks, all of its demands, and then we have to figure out how to live with it.

Living with a business doesn't mean the same thing to every woman. The owner-manager's wife is in a much different situation from the successor's wife. Daughters-in-law are not daughters, a fact usually made obvious to them constantly.

Widows are not wives. They face an entirely different set of questions, all defined by a business they may or may not understand.

How do we learn to live with loneliness? How do we learn to handle the fact that our husbands seem to spend more time on the job than they do at home? How do we manage all of the conflict the business generates between Dad and all of his heirs—successors and non-successors—as well as between Dad and their mates? How, too, do we live with competition from the business for Dad's attention?

A LIFE OF DILEMMAS

One very subtle effect of business ownership is that it puts us—or seems to put us—in the difficult position of having to work at odds with each other to achieve what we all want.

A good example is the following story a young woman told me about the jog she took with her husband that same morning. I've tried to stick to her words as closely as possible:

"Jason and I took up jogging a couple of years ago as a good way of exercising together," she told me. "This morning we were out there on the beach, and I started out with my typical burst of energy. Right away, I was yards ahead of him.

"I know why I took the lead—I'm younger than he is and a lot lighter, but it still gave me a real sense of elation to be sprinting ahead.

"As usual, Jason's strength and endurance—not to mention his competitiveness—overcame my eagerness and he moved out ahead, getting a fairly good-sized lead.

"Well, we passed a few people standing on the edge of the beach. I was about 20 feet behind Jason, and as I passed those people, I heard one of them remark, 'Look at her, she'll *never* catch him.'

"My immediate reaction was to get mad at them—and at Jason, too. I started to push myself to run faster and harder to catch him and *beat* him.

"Then, maybe because of the beautiful sunrise or the salt air or just my common sense, it suddenly occurred to me that there wasn't any reason why I had to be in direct competition with Jason. His beating me at jogging didn't make me less than he was. We weren't even supposed to be racing.

"In fact, the whole point was to be doing something *together*.

"I've given that trip down the beach a lot of thought, and I think it represents something really important.

"Sometimes it's good to run alongside each other. At other times, it may be the best thing to take different paths. Having a common goal doesn't mean we have to use the same paths to get there. It's necessary, sometimes, and even enjoyable to run the way we want, at our own paces.

"But what is so easy to forget is that we should be doing things together even if we're not doing them the same way. There's so much competition in the world already that if we start competing with our mates, we stand to lose one of the best supporters we have."

Another woman I met at that same program, who was older than Jane by some 20 years, and had a husband who was approaching retirement, said it a different way:

"Caring and working to make things better is what marriage is all about. It's important for us to concentrate on our own individual potential and needs, but it's also absolutely essential to stay tuned into each other, to always look outward at the world together."

Of course, this is true for marriage in general. But the family business adds a whole basket full of new problems to the burden every one of us already carries into our future. Often, the women in family businesses find themselves cast into this role of making sure that *everybody* "runs together" at their own paces.

WE STAND BETWEEN GENERATIONS

Quite often, we mothers find ourselves in the necessary, but uncomfortable position of mediator between our husbands and our children.

I remember the case of a good friend of ours whose son, and only child, had planned for years to be a lawyer. She and her husband accepted his decision, and they encouraged him in every way they could, although they were a little disappointed because they'd hoped he would join them in their successful business.

While their son was in law school, our friend's husband had a serious stroke which abruptly ended his career.

The son, knowing how important the business was to his parents' security, made the difficult decision to quit law school and help them run the business. They reluctantly agreed.

Needless to say, this sudden transition faced a lot of problems. The son was intelligent and aggressive enough, but he had never learned much about the business.

As far as the employees, the suppliers, and the customers were concerned, he was an unknown. He made a lot of mistakes in the beginning, some of them fairly serious, but he hung on with determination and worked to make the business succeed.

As if these problems weren't enough for him, his father, who'd been forced without preparation to give up his physical business life, wasn't quite ready, mentally, to allow himself to be supplanted. He became highly critical of his son's performance.

And, as usual, poor Mom got caught in the middle. Her husband often thought that she was taking the side of "her" son. On the other hand, their son chafed under his father's stubbornness and often felt that his parents weren't giving him the freedom he needed to manage effectively.

She understood her husband's despair and frustration at being suddenly confined to a wheelchair after a lifetime of activity and accomplishment.

She also understood the unselfish commitment their son had made, changing his career plans in order to fill in the vacuum his father's illness had left.

She understood, too, the great love each man had for the other. So she concentrated her energies on keeping as much peace between the two as she could, day by day, week by week.

What made her job even tougher was the constant misunderstanding of her actions by both men. Many times, she bore the brunt of their anger and frustration with each other, because she was the target of convenience.

Eventually, very slowly, the heir began to get a firm control over the business. He earned the confidence of the employees, the suppliers, and the customers. He got the business back on a positive growth curve and gained the respect of his father.

But all of this took time, and had the feud between father and son gone unmediated, that time just wouldn't have been available.

It took a very strong, patient woman to help guide that transition, someone who loved both men, someone who understood them and could cope with their mutual frustrations. The IRS may not believe we deserve salaries, but maybe that just goes to show that some of the most valuable things in life can't be bought at any price.

WE HAVE TO UNDERSTAND

Still, even the strongest person has to know what the problems are before those problems can be addressed. A mediator who doesn't know the issues at stake will be more a *cause* than a solution to problems. But even women who don't have to mediate must face the facts and problems of life in the family business, each for her own reasons.

The owner's wife needs information to be able to support her husband's struggles with the "baby" he created, as well as to be able to fight whatever she needs to fight.

The successor's wife, too, must know what's going on around her so that she can come to some realistic conclusions about what's happening to her husband and their future. She will be constantly exposed to a successor who seems always frustrated and discouraged, and she will wonder why her father-in-law seems oblivious to what he's doing to his son. How can she know what's really happening—and how can she be of help, rather than becoming an unknowing agitator?

For family members actively involved in the business, the problem may not be so great because they are in a position to know what's happening. But what, for example, about the business owner's daughters, the successor's sisters, who are living out of town? What can they think or say when their husbands point out how much their brothers are taking out of the business while they receive nothing?

What about the poor widow who was never allowed to know anything and now finds that her entire future is in the hands of some unknown banker administering a trust she doesn't understand? What about the second wife of the Boss, who not only isn't cut in on what's happening in the business, but, because she's "trying to take Mom's place," is so typically cut out of ever really knowing or understanding the Boss's kids, the successors?

HOW DO WE LEARN?

I seem to hear the same question over and over again... "how can I get my husband to tell me what's going on?"

I really don't have a simple formula; but I've received some ideas that might help.

Usually, the woman who is home all day with little children seems to have the greatest need to discuss things with her husband—probably because she has an overwhelming need for adult conversation.

The communication problem doesn't *seem* to be so urgent for working wives, probably because both partners have the stimulation of others all day; but, because neither partner then pushes to get the necessary talking done, this situation can be even worse.

Many times a woman can be so involved in her own activities that her need to keep doing what she's doing can slam the door on any sort of change within the business. It's important for her to realize what's needed for the success of a family business and how that's going to affect what she wants to do.

Let's concentrate, for the moment, on the woman who is not actively employed outside the home. She is, by far, in the majority.

A housewife/mother can be so starved for some adult companionship that she'll meet her husband at the door and deluge him with questions about the office, frequently even before he gets his feet in the house.

This is more common among younger women, who haven't yet been pushed away so often that they give up. Since Dad doesn't understand what his wife needs from him, and since what he wants most is some time to "relax," he brushes her off. His answer, most likely, is "I don't feel like talking shop."

She, on the other hand, is so immersed in her needs that she isn't able to stand in his shoes and give him some time to unwind. The result is often silence, resentment, and conflict.

This is why wives of business owners so frequently almost take a pride in their lack of interest in the business. They are insulating themselves against hurt. This is why successors' wives become bitter and react angrily whenever the business is brought up. They have been made to feel like outsiders.

And, too, given time, this is why so many widows spend their remaining years in anxiety and confusion.

It shouldn't happen. It can't be allowed to happen. In fact, I think we'd be wise to consider our need to find out what's happening as a life or death matter. We will suffer the most if this thing is swept under the rug.

Many women have refused to remain ignorant. I've already mentioned the young woman who always had a hot bath waiting for her husband when he got home. She'd wait a while for the hot water to dissolve his tension. Then, when she figured he was loose enough, she'd climb into the tub with the two martinis.

Against a one-two punch like that, the poor old boy didn't have a chance. He *relaxed*—and she certainly got his attention. They learned to talk.

Maybe your husband doesn't like hot water or martinis, but I think you get the idea. Anyone who's been working in a fast-paced, demanding world all day needs to unwind before anything else. First things first. Later we talk.

If we want to be realistic, we probably should accept the fact that our husband *is* tired when he gets home. We should accept the probability that rehashing what he's just gone through won't be high on his list of favorite things.

After all, he's been talking all day—arguing, negotiating, selling, buying—and he's tired of that. Who wouldn't be? He may thrive on it all, but that doesn't mean it doesn't wear him out.

So, someone has to take the initiative to keep the conversation flowing. If we're the ones who need it and miss it, then the responsibility—in fact, if not in justice—falls on us. A good start might be coming right out and saying we need to know, but, after that, a little creativity will probably be needed.

Remember that our husbands don't really want aggressive inquisitors or clever consultants. What they think they need are sympathetic listeners. But we know they need a little bit more. They need sympathetic listeners who can supply a unique wisdom all their own.

In order to live with our family businesses, we have to understand as much as we can about those businesses. But this isn't all. Not only do we need to know about the business—it could also be (just maybe) that there are a lot of things we have to tell our husbands about ourselves and what we're doing...

ⵣⵣⵣⵣⵣⵣⵣⵣⵣ

Surviving
and
Thriving
Day to Day

Chapter 4

A Boss We Also Sleep With

Wives have long had significant roles in their family businesses. If anything, this trend is increasing, especially since there has been such an expansion in that group called "daughter-successors." Every day, we're going to be seeing more women owner-managers, not the "woman Friday" but the "woman Boss" of the successful family business.

The working woman faces a whole range of important questions, many of them added to, and most of them totally unlike those faced by women who aren't directly involved in their businesses.

Betty, for example, has been an involved and vital part of the management of their company since she and her husband bought it. When I asked her whether she ever regretted her decision to work with her husband, she told me she hadn't, ever. Here is how she described her experience:

"Naturally we have our day-to-day problems, but then what kind of life doesn't? Our problems have always been far outweighed by the joys and rewards, and I love the business. I love what it's done for our family.

"The gift isn't without a price, of course. I developed an ulcer, so I can't pretend business pressures weren't part of the problem. I worked hard for that ulcer; guess I really earned it, but thanks to medical research and an acceptance of the need to relax, it's been eliminated completely.

"But even with that, I have no regrets. I feel great now."

I asked her what kind of affect working with and for her husband had on her marriage, and she firmly believed it was positive.

"We couldn't work together better than we do," she told me, "mostly I think, because we're still very much in love and thoroughly enjoy each other's company after 30 years of marriage.

"Walt has always shown total respect for my opinions and business judgement and he's given me complete responsibility in my own areas of expertise. In a business, even love can't make up for a lack of mutual respect.

"He's a financial person, both in education and experience, and in my opinion he's a business genius. On the other hand, I'm people-oriented, creative, and an idea person. So for me personnel, public relations, sales and advertising came naturally.

"Walt and I have made a great team. I think it's because our interests and preferences are so different that we are so compatible in the business.

"We're together almost every day, for breakfast, lunch and dinner. That's why I can't relate to business owners' wives who feel left out, neglected or patronized. I know there are many who feel that way, but our situation just isn't like that.

"Even with all the time we spend together, Walt and I still get away together often, just to be alone without the business—just us. Oh, how we cherish those times!

"I've got to do it, though. Periodically, I just tell Walt where we're going and when. I have the reservations and arrangements all made. He likes this, and it works beautifully."

THE WORKING DAUGHTERS

One of the more unique aspects of Betty's business is the fact that her two daughters are working in the company, something neither she nor Walt had really contemplated 16 years ago when they bought the business.

"We never thought about it back then," she recalled. "It wasn't actually rejected or accepted as an idea. It just never came up. But am I ever pleased it's worked out this way.

"I'll always remember one night about four years ago when our older daughter came home one evening after attending one of your summer seminars in Cleveland.

"Walt was out of town, so I was totally in charge of the company. When Judy came in, she found me still in my office late on a Friday night. I know I looked haggard and worn, because I was struggling with a number of important problems.

"Instead of greeting her, I blurted out my frustration: 'I'll sure be glad when your father gets back. If anything ever happens to him...'

"Judy immediately put her arm around me and said, 'If anything ever happens to Dad, don't worry, Mom. *We'll* run this place!'

"Needless to say, I was surprised. But, you know, I *believed* her!"

Walt and Betty seem to work together beautifully. With their two daughters actively and very responsibly involved in the business, the entire family has now pulled themselves together into an effective and vital team.

"We like to think," Betty said, "that our two daughters could take hold and become important parts of the management of the business, because Walt and I raised them into the company in a very professional, business-like way.

"Each has her own area of responsibility and expertise, and each is totally involved. Their enthusiasm for their work is almost overwhelming, and they work together beautifully.

"I think if you asked them why, their first answer would be because we believe in them and they know it. In the business world, with a father-mother-daughter-daughter situation, that's not an easy relationship to establish.

"We've given them definite areas of great responsibility because we have complete faith in their abilities. They've responded to our confidence with dedication and hard work.

"I don't mean to imply that we don't have business differences, but we're always careful to keep the differences 'business' and not let anything personal slip in. It's hard to do this, but it's essential to a healthy family life."

CHILDREN IMPLY IN-LAWS

Betty and Walt have given a lot of thought to the future, and with daughters, an important part of that future is the potential son-in-law/successor. One of the girls is married to an accountant with a national firm. He's very much like Walt, and they often talk shop. Betty said she would really be surprised if he didn't someday want to join their business. She knew Walt would really enjoy the association—and the help. Their younger daughter, too, is so convinced having her husband work in the business would be a good idea, she's even talking it over with her fiancee.

Had Betty and Walt had sons instead of daughters, they would be facing another question—should their daughters-in-law get involved in the family company? Our sons marry. This seems to be a fact of life which we couldn't—and wouldn't—change. But do we want those young women working in *our* business? It's not an easy question for many people to answer, particularly Dad, who'd often prefer to see the mother of his grandchildren actually "mother" his grandchildren. There's more to be said on this subject in the chapters on the daughter-in-law.

Families don't expand without tension, especially if those families also own and manage businesses. Betty has experienced the pressures involved with keeping a family in business together, trying to act as a combination mother, manager, and wife. Putting these roles together tends to give Mom's job some new and interesting wrinkles, so there's a real wisdom to be gained in the kind of experience she's had.

THE WORKING PEACEMAKER

"I've learned a few things over the years," she said. "Maybe I should have known them before, but I guess I'm a slow learner. For example, in a family-owned business like ours, someone in the family must surely act as a peacemaker— sometimes even a peace-initiator. And to be totally honest, I believe that that's my most important responsibility.

"We work together well and we get along—but ideas and opinions are bound to clash. We all realize from the outset that we have to agree to agree, but sometimes some very firm reminders are needed. That's where I come in.

"Walt and I agree that every organization—whether it's a family, a business, or whatever—works best with one leader in both our business and our family. Walt fills that role.

"But I also know that the success of our family and our business is due in large part to my influence, over and above my competence in my job. Walt is the patriarch in the family and the president of the company. He's the boss and that's fine with me. I have the respect and confidence of my family and the people I work with and that means more to me than being the boss or having a title.

"It's a good life."

TOGETHERNESS IS LEARNED

This last sentiment is shared by so many women I've met. They've been through the problems and the fears, but all in all, looking back, almost every one of them wouldn't change a thing. In some marriages, of course, working together in business can lead to intolerable strains. But it's been my experience that more frequently, a husband and wife working together can wind up with a *stronger* marriage—and a more successful business.

For example, Shirley and her husband work together in their business now as partners, but it wasn't always an equal arrangement. They didn't always share everything. Building the team wasn't always that smooth. It took the two of them some time to realize that working together meant understanding together.

An increasing number of married couples are dreaming of working together in a business they own, something Shirley and her husband, Brian, managed to do. Shirley believes this should be encouraged, based on her own experience. But, she pointed out to me, that wasn't the advice they got years ago when they first started.

"I can't count the number of people who told us that we would never make it working so closely," she said proudly, "but it looks like we've proven them wrong."

Shirley and Brian have a mutual interest—the company— and a mutual goal—seeing it grow and prosper. They work hard to achieve that, and both feel that the business—and their marriage—wouldn't be what it is today if they hadn't worked together.

"In the long run," she said, "it's been a great thing. We've both grown and matured with our business. We've kept pace with each other and we always seem to move in the same direction."

But, as you might suspect, things weren't always so happy. In Shirley's own words:

"Brian started the company right after we got married 15 years ago and, in those days, the business was really struggling.

"While I was home, though, things seemed to be going along very smoothly. Brian worked hard, of course, and seemed tired a lot, but I assumed that was normal when someone was building a business.

"Then, five years later, when I came to work with Brian, he didn't seem to want me to know anything about the financial end of the business. He taught me how to handle shipping and purchasing and payroll and all that, and I got to the point I could manage almost any of the inside work. But the inner secrets of the business stayed off limits.

"Still, going to work with him was an absolute revelation. I always believed Brian and I communicated very well, but once I got involved in the business, I realized I only heard what he thought I should hear.

"Eventually I started learning my way around the company. I began to feel like I was developing a sixth sense. Even without Brian telling me, I learned which orders were important, what the consequences of production delays were, and what the loss of an expected sale meant.

"Most important, as I learned, I not only saw the problems, I began to feel responsible for them. They were no longer Brian's problems alone. They were *ours*. Brian may have felt that he was still carrying the burden alone, but I knew otherwise."

Shirley didn't really understand why Brian felt he had to keep everything to himself. She didn't believe the common idea that a new business is like a founder's mistress, someone he has to keep as a deep, dark secret. The closest she could come was her feeling that Brian was afraid to admit his failures.

This was the point around which she decided to launch her campaign.

"I decided early in the game that Brian had to be convinced he could tell me of his failures as well as his successes, daily, without thinking he was losing stature in my eyes," she said.

"But I also knew that I was going to have to learn when to let him alone with his thoughts and problems. That was the hard part for me, but I knew what I was expecting from Brian was going to be hard for him, too.

"The business may have been Brian's secret possession when he founded it," she told me, "but I couldn't accept that. Today I'd have to say it's more like another of our children, someone we've suffered over and raised together. We're both very proud of what our business has grown to be, and we're willing to share all of the good and bad with each other.

"And the key factor was that we learned to talk."

What seems certain from the working wives I've known, is that while working together is not for everyone, for those who can make it work, there are rewards that far outweigh the effort involved.

AWARENESS MUST COME EARLY

If a woman feels she wants to share in this strange and mysterious pursuit called her husband's business, the major problem she faces is getting that sharing to happen soon enough. If she waits too long, eventually it gets too late to come together at all.

It may well be that some husbands have an emotional *need* for their wives to be ignorant (or at least to act that way), because it allows them to feel superior. And I also know some women are bored speechless by "business talk." They need to feel protected and taken care of.

But if a couple really wants to work together, they're going to have to understand together.

And this has to begin very early. In Shirley's case, it's obvious if Brian had to start today trying to help her understand the business, it would be an almost impossible job. There aren't enough hours in the day to make up for years of missed experience.

I can't emphasize too strongly how important I think this is. If a couple haven't made a practice of talking about the impact the business makes on their personal lives—their hopes and their plans, their values and their price—then every effort should be made to begin—now, before it's too late.

Remember, it wasn't raining when Noah built the Ark.

CRECECECECECE

Chapter 5

Mom Can Own It, Too

We today see an ever-increasing number of women who are founding and managing their own businesses. But even so, the female business *founder* is a relatively rare breed. Women who own family businesses are not so rare, however. While some of them—an increasing number—are trained successors, too many women business owners find themselves owners of businesses they neither founded nor knew how to run.

There are three ways women can become business owners without being founders. Probably the most common situation is one in which a woman inherits a business from her husband—a widow's blessing that can often turn into a widow's bane. The second is for a daughter to inherit a business as the successor to her father. The third is for a daughter to inherit the business, while the management of the company is handled by others.

THE "GORILLA'S WIFE"

Martha is a good example of this last situation. As the daughter of a business founder, she's been the sole owner of their family construction company since her father's death seventeen years ago. Her other sister wanted no part of the business, and was pleased to get her residual share of the estate in property and investments.

Although ownership is held entirely by Martha, she's not involved in the management of the company. She was a business owner's daughter married to the "boss-in-being," and it was her husband, Mickey, who became president of the company after her Dad died.

I asked her what was unusual about being in that position, and she told me there were a lot of things.

"Dad used to kid Mickey about being the 'gorilla in bed with his baby,'" she said, "and I can tell you that the role of 'Baby'—in my case, the daughter/inheritor married to the 'gorilla' turned business son—is very difficult.

"At least it was very difficult for me. So many women today object if society tries to identify them by association with their husbands, but Mickey and I faced the opposite problem at a time when such a situation was certainly less common. The only models I had to follow were famous movie actresses with *their* husbands.

"The sensitivity of the male ego, combined with my generations's lack of 'liberation' created a situation that was rough for everybody. Everywhere we went, for example, my husband wasn't Mickey. He was 'Martha's husband.'

"That was a very hard thing for him, particularly among the people he worked with in the company. Remembering that many of these employees had known me since childhood didn't always make it easier."

Martha wasn't comfortable with her role, either. In fact, most women of her generation probably wouldn't be. She knew Mickey would prove himself over time by demonstrating his leadership, but she also realized that there was a great deal she had to do to help change the situation. After all, she seemed to be getting all the attention.

One of the most important factors, she feels, was that Mickey and she respected each other and could agree how they were going to share their lives—the traditional roles of her generation, his as husband, father, and provider; hers as wife, mother, and general keeper of the family.

"Since we had this worked out between us," she said, "eventually the outside world began to get the message, too. But we didn't manage that overnight. It took years."

Not only were these the problems faced while Mickey was the "successor-in-training," but when Martha's father passed away, leaving her the business and Mickey the presidency, additional adjustments had to be made.

"In many ways," Martha told me, "we were back at square one. Now I had the power of ownership and it seemed as if all the attention was again focusing on me.

"It was a sensitive issue, and it took a while to reverse the attitudes I kept running into. I had to make it clear to everybody that Mickey was the boss, that I stood behind him, and that every good thing happening for the company was due to *his* efforts.

"Looking back, I can see what a potentially explosive situation we were in. If a husband and wife didn't get along in this kind of a fix, it could be disastrous for the business.

"Fortunately we continued to agree on our respective roles in business and family, so it all worked out. Oh, things didn't go all that smoothly, but it was more like smoothing the rough edges than repaving the road."

Actually, Mickey's situation is as difficult as Martha's, and she sees a number of differences between him and the typical owner-manager.

For one thing, Mickey's attitude toward the company was different. Unlike a founder-president, he didn't create the business. It was always right there in front of him that someday his wife—not he—would be the owner. That's a big difference, and, in many ways, Martha believes it's been helpful.

"I think Mickey has been much more open to constructive criticism and the advice of objective advisors than Dad ever was," she said. "He doesn't take it so personally, so he can respond more quickly and positively. I think this has been a big factor in the tremendous growth the business has had under Mickey's leadership.

"Another major difference was on the negative side. Any major problems Mickey wanted to discuss with me most likely concerned *my* family, *my* father, *my* sister, *my* mother, and Mickey realized I was smack in the middle between my family and him.

"This made for some difficult discussions, and I know there were many times Mickey simply kept quiet about problems to avoid upsetting me.

"A wife can often be a valuable sounding board for her husband's business problems, but this was something of a dilemma for us when Dad was still president. I know there were many times Mickey had to swallow his frustrations because his boss was my father."

(Martha didn't mention another problem sons-in-law and their fathers-in-law often face—the problem of equity. It can be quite natural for a competent young man to want to have some of the equity of the business he's helping to build in his own name. But Dad faces the dilemma of wondering if the "gorilla" is really going to stay with "Baby." What if Dad gives the kid some stock in his own name, and then he...??)

"Dad, on the other hand, wasn't quite as sensitive to my position as Mickey was. As much as he respected my husband, he'd seem to test my comparative loyalty to each of them. Many times when he and Mickey were at odds about something (and he knew I knew it), Dad would ask my opinion.

"What could I say? I always made every effort to see both points of view. I loved both of them and wanted to help, but it was a rough situation.

"Usually, my sentiments sided with Mickey because we think alike and, well, I suppose I'm biased. But even when I didn't agree, I'd pretty much keep quiet about it. After all, my first love and loyalty was—and is—with my husband. I could only hope that Dad and Mom would understand my position.

"I couldn't expect them to necessarily like or agree with it, but I hoped they understood. Now that both of them are gone, a lot of the problem is too, but some residue remains. Mickey and I still don't discuss the business and what it means to us as much as we should."

DAD'S DAUGHTER-SUCCESSOR

Not too long ago, the thought that a daughter could inherit and run a family company—other than, maybe, a boutique or some other "frilly" business—was seldom entertained by business owners. If we had daughters, we expected them to marry nice boys and raise lovely grandchildren. If anybody would work in the business, it would be their husbands, our sons-in-law.

The times are changing, and we should be grateful for that. Our successor seminars, which used to be 99.9% male, are now approaching an almost complete integration. Our daughters are becoming actively interested in careers as owner-managers, and in industries which up to now were considered masculine domains.

Women-successors share many of the problems and challenges their brother-counterparts face, of course, but there are some major differences. Daughters have different relationships with their fathers, for example, often far less competitive than the relationship sons have with their fathers.

But daughters have a much greater problem being taken seriously, not only by Dad, but also by the employees and by suppliers or customers. It somehow seems much easier to give real responsibility to a son, maybe because he seems so much more "serious" about the business than his sister could ever be. Maybe, too, we worry about our daughter-successor marrying an ambitious, fast-rising—and very mobile—executive in a major public company. What happens when his career transfers him out of town? Where does our carefully trained successor go?

It can happen. It has happened. But, then, there are many possible disasters. If we plan to avoid them all, we wind up planning nothing of any consequence. Over the years, I've met many young women who are planning on staying with their family businesses and growing with them. They are every bit as smart, aggressive, and competent as their brothers—without losing that elusive quality that makes them women.

THE ENTRAPPED WIDOW

And then there is the widow who's never worked with her husband, and who finds herself left with a business she is not prepared to understand, but which represents both her husband's greatest achievement and her future security.

Professionals who've been involved in the planning of many estates, who've also seen the results of many of these plans, too often see a discrepancy between what Dad wanted to happen and what he put on the paper.

Many mistakes are made in estate planning, but probably the most tragic involves the situation where a son, son-in-law, a daughter, or multiple successors take over the management of a business Dad has left to Mother. One of the saddest things to watch is mothers and children who've generally gotten along, grow apart because they're trapped in a situation they can't control.

Leaving the business to a wife who doesn't understand that business, despite all of Dad's good intentions, is usually an estate planning disaster. Independent of the tax consequences, which others can explain far better than I, the worst result is the fact that while Mom may own the business, she'll find it next to impossible to get much real benefit from it.

In most cases, she can't get much of a salary. Remember, I'm talking about a woman who has had little to do with the business. When Dad dies, most often his wife is in her sixties and either has never worked in the business, or worked so long ago it doesn't count. In these circumstances, it's almost impossible to justify giving her a salary of any consequence—especially a salary commensurate with the high income she and Dad were used to.

The tax people are going to get very upset if, suddenly, we give a 65-year-old widow with no business experience a significant salary. The IRS would call that a dividend, not salary, and dividends cost a lot more in taxes—at least in the United States.

Typically, Dad assumes he's protecting his wife by giving her all the stock in the business. This, he reasons, will make sure the kids will take care of her. While this sounds very good, the nature of the situation instead puts Mom in the position of becoming a thorn in her children's sides. She's always trying to get the money she needs—and is entitled to—but the successors have few ways to get it to her without a greater cost than than they are willing, or able, to pay.

The problem is not so much the successor's lack of willingness to take care of his mother as it is the fact that his hands are financially tied. He's not greedy, necessarily, just very short of options.

If he is well trained and really good at what he does, if he is able to succeed at it, he should enjoy the fruits of his success. We've seen many good businesses that mushroomed even further when the second generation took over. And it's right that our successors should enjoy these rewards.

But, to be fair about this, if that successor isn't capable and fails, he shouldn't be able to pull Mother down with him. However it's done technically, experience has shown over and over that estate plans should be designed so that Mother is taken care of independently of the business.

The experts tell me that there are a number of options. (I present these as examples, not as suggestions. Technical solutions change constantly with the tax laws.)

For one, Dad could set up a trust for Mom during his lifetime, funded through insurance paid for by the business. On his death, a sizeable sum of cash would be put into trust for her, a sum they agreed upon together. This money belongs exclusively to her. She has the principal and income to live on, and she is, in fact, divorced from the business, because the stock is in the hands of the successors.

A second arrangement could be for Dad, during his lifetime to take some of his common stock and put it into preferred stock that carries a dividend. Another option is perhaps to exchange stock for some kind of debt that can be willed to Mom so the business can pay her interest. The important thing is to give her adequate income without requiring that she be actively involved in the business.

A third option, which depends upon the nature of the business, would be to take certain assets—frequently the real estate—which can be segregated from the business itself and treat it separately. It's fairly common for business owners to own the real estate personally and separately from the stock in the business.

Then he can leave his wife the real estate, having the business support Mom through rental income.

Estate planning doesn't have to be one-sided so that if it's advantageous to one party, another has to suffer. It's very possible to put these things in balance so they work together. The important consideration is to put control of the business where it belongs, with those managing the business, while providing adequately for the widow of the business owner.

I've seen many times how the trusting wife who doesn't want to be included in estate planning can become the fearful widow forced into living under a plan she doesn't understand. To leave her out is unfair to her—and ultimately unfair to the successors.

Everyone wants to see Mom taken care of. In fact, successors are usually nicer to their mothers when Mom's financial problems aren't all entwined with business problems. Good estate planning can avoid this, allowing our children to be more generous and get along much better with their mothers.

It's the *lack* of planning that lays the seeds of conflict.

ᘎᘎᘎᘎᘎᘎᘎᘎᘎᘎᘎ

Chapter 6

We Make Lousy Directors

Many years ago Léon decided that his business needed a working board of outside directors. He explained to me then why he didn't want me as a director. He said he could always find directors, but he only had one wife and he didn't want a directorship to clutter up a fine relationship.

We've always enjoyed good communications, and since I wasn't active in the business, I didn't feel a really great need to sit on the board, anyway.

Five years later, Léon and I were in a terrible airplane accident. I was in a state of shock, and he was severely injured. All at once, many of life's simple and routine things seemed overwhelming. Something as uncomplicated as dealing with an unpleasant ambulance company became too much to handle.

Our directors took over all such burdens. They were right there, ready to help me in any way.

At first I was relieved. But as the shock wore off, I found that even though I had great help available, I was starting to panic because neither my husband nor I was running the business. I also discovered that I didn't know enough about our business to run it even if I had to.

The need was obvious: I had to learn more about the business.

So after Léon's recovery, we decided to do something about this. A good approach seemed to be including me as a regular *guest* at all board meetings. This way I could not only get to know more about the business, I would also become better acquainted with the directors.

The first couple of meetings I attended were a little hard on all of us. I think I had a kind of dampening effect on the proceedings, making the directors feel uncomfortable giving my husband the honest and *direct* advice he needed.

It was probably even harder for me to keep my emotions under control whenever the directors disagreed with him. But time has a way of working these things out, and soon the benefits began appearing.

As an invited guest to the board meetings, for example, I receive the agenda in advance. This gives me an opportunity to see what will be discussed, so I can then sit down with my husband before the meeting and ask him questions and express my concerns.

Sometimes, too, at the board meetings my husband will bring up problems that are worrying him, but which he hasn't discussed with me. This helps him remember his promise to share his problems with me.

There is another good reason for me to attend the meetings. Should something happen to him, not only will I know how things are being run, but I'll know his future plans as well.

And, I'll know his board members—the people who are most able and willing to aid me in crises—well enough to be comfortable with them—and they with me.

As far as I'm concerned, sitting *in* as a guest at the meetings has more advantages than sitting *on* the board as a director.

DIRECTORS ARE SPECIAL PEOPLE

I'm now an active officer of our company. I'm also a shareholder, and the wife of the president. But I don't feel that gives me the right to sit on the board of directors.

Before you start to object, as I know many of you will, let me explain why I think this way.

My husband, like most successful business owners, is an extremely powerful man in his own right. It's important for him to be able to surround himself with intelligent people who are not afraid to say "you are wrong," people he respects, who can give him help when issues get clouded with emotion or dreams, and fantasy with facts.

I don't need to be on the board to give my husband the help I have to give, and, besides, I don't feel that I qualify as a director, because, even though I know about "our" business, I haven't really seen the inside workings of any other businesses. My opinion is based more on intuition than on observation.

Even though I'm intelligent, full of ideas, and not afraid to speak my mind, I am not a risk-taking peer to my husband. It does neither of us much good to take a first-class wife and make her into a second-class director.

Of course, as a wife and (according to the actuaries) an eventual inheritor, I have a very definite right to know where the company is going. I also have the right to know the directors beyond a nodding acquaintance, as well as to have them know me and my views.

But I don't need to be a *director* to understand and be understood. These things should come to me in other ways, as my husband's wife and life partner. If they don't, no directorship is going to make up for a communication problem at home.

ONLY DIRECTORS WHO DIRECT

Many people believe that the board is designed for their use in looking out for their interests. This is why there are so many directors who are minority shareholder relatives of the owner-manager. This explains the brothers-in-law who "represent" the sisters of The Boss. This is why many widows sit on boards, or have trust officers to "look out for their interests." This is also why every investor who ever put $10 into the company in the early days thinks he deserves a board seat to watch over "his money."

All these people do is watch operating management and the involved family members to make sure they don't steal from what these "investors" consider to be "their" business. If there isn't more faith than that in the people managing the company, the problems go a lot deeper than questions of who's sitting on the board.

These "outsiders" are worried because they have little control over an investment which they see only as a potential source of unearned income. While this is understandable, it is an unstable situation. These people are, in fact, "prisoners" to a investment that's not designed as an investment. The solution to this problem is not expanding representation on the board. The solution is freeing the prisoners, finding some way to liquidate their interest and putting it in a form that better fits their needs.

Directors are supposed to *direct*. There's nothing in any corporate charter that says a director should make sure that he gets his before others get theirs. Directors are charged with preserving the strength, profitability, and growth of the company they direct. This is based on the assumption that what's good for the company is good for the owners. In most cases, this is true.

It's true that there can be many people interested very intimately in the management of the business and how it's run.

But "representation" on the board is not going to guarantee the quality of that management. The only true representation in a family company is in a contribution to its growth and well being. Mere presence on the board often will guarantee little other than leaving less room for a more qualified person.

The board of our company is composed of five outsiders and my husband. I attend each meeting as a guest, and I consider my attendance to be important.

I come to the meetings familiar with the agenda. I've thought it through and usually discussed it with my husband. When I feel it's necessary, I voice my opinions and concerns forcefully, but concisely.

Though I'm not a director, I'm actively involved in the board meetings. I feel that my opinions carry weight and that I know exactly where the company is headed. I'm also confident that these men, whom I've come to know well, are qualified and will be responsible for seeing that our company continues should tragedy strike it or my husband. They are men who know what they are doing and who understand my desires and needs.

These same directors—or people like them—can also understand the needs and concerns of others, particularly non-involved family members who are minority shareholders.

Our taking a seat on that board would just mean one less person of director caliber available to help our husbands, our brothers, or the successors—whoever they may be.

I'd prefer to think of us as "directors-at-large." Our husband can have our help and advice whenever they need it, but that's not true with the advice of their risk-taking peers, those people whose help is best made available only through the structure of the board meetings.

FEAR IS NATURAL

I'm not a director of our company because, to my way of thinking, I'm a great deal more. Still, I'm not about to imply that this decision was a simple one to reach. I've had many doubts of my own, many times when I felt that maybe I really should be a director after all.

For example, Léon and I have always had a super arrangement for communicating with each other. We have always managed—by talking—to translate "his" hopes and dreams into "ours."

So it was *together* that we decided to share our plans for the future with a board of outside directors. We also decided, together, that it would be a good idea to formalize the board's role in running the company should my husband be unable to continue managing it himself.

Our way of doing that was for him to write a "letter of intent" asking that the board accept the responsibility for assuring continuing management of the company in the event he couldn't. I thoroughly understood and agreed with the decision.

This was all discussed at the next board meeting, where we asked the directors if they were willing to accept this responsibility. They all said they were. They thought it was an excellent idea and seemed very willing, so a resolution was passed to have the letter of intent written to the board. I didn't think much more about the matter.

Then came "Blue Thursday," a day when I'd locked my keys in the car, the painter ran one roll short of a wallpaper I'd spent weeks selecting (and which turned out to be discontinued), Léon had been away all week, and I had no one to talk to.

That happened, also, to be the day the minutes of the board meeting arrived.

I read the minutes, and when I came to the paragraph describing the letter of intent, Blue Thursday turned purple. Although I had agreed to the decision intellectually, I suddenly found myself hitting the emotional panic button.

Suddenly, that letter of intent seemed to mean that the board would control "our" business, that I would have nothing to say about "our" dream. I was not one of "them," and I saw that letter as a threat to my independence. Blue Thursday was complete...and it was a disaster.

Well, thank God that Friday follows Thursday. The next day dawned bright and sunny, and a good night's sleep helped me put everything in perspective. I remembered what I guess I always knew. Our directors *do* understand our dream. They *do* listen to what I have to say, and they *are* very concerned for my independence.

But this whole experience made me stop and wonder. If this kind of fear can happen to a wife who *is* included in the plans for the future, who does share equally in business dreams, I can only fear for those women who do not have these advantages.

My conclusion? There's no such thing as over-communication. We can seldom know too much. Blue Thursdays are hard enough without having ignorance to add to our fears.

It may be up to us to understand, but it's also up to our husbands, their advisors and especially their directors—actually *our* directors—to do everything they can to help us understand, as well as to make sure we feel comfortable with the plans that are being made for our future.

CXXXXXXXXXXX

The Next Generation of "Managers"

Chapter 7

We're Raising Rich Kids

Raising our children is one of the most important and difficult jobs we'll ever have. It's a job we all accept even though we usually have very little experience and absolutely no formal training.

If we own a business, that job, because of the added implications, is even bigger and more important. A successful business means wealth, power, and freedom, including the oftentimes unfortunate apparent freedom from the need for personal discipline.

Although life may be hard enough for all children, it becomes impossible if the child doesn't understand what inheriting material success can mean, particularly if that child is not prepared to accept the responsibilities that go with the privileges.

How do we teach our children and grandchildren this responsibility, both financial and personal? We are, after all, raising rich kids.

Many readers might bristle at that last sentence, but that underlines a major cause of the problem. We know how hard we are struggling to keep everything together, and we know who the *really* rich people are—we've met them. "Rich" takes on its own meaning in the eyes of the beholder.

But remember, too, that the waitress at the restaurant, the person who helps clean our house, the people working in the office or in the shop, all think that *we* are rich. And we shouldn't fight that. We *are* rich in the sense that we've put together significant resources, and, as such, we make up a very small percentage of the population.

No matter how "rich" is defined, and how much more some people may have, it is a fact that the children of successful business owners have privileges and resources which are greater than those available to most other children. So, whether we like to admit it or not, we must face the fact that we are raising rich kids.

But wealth is not a windfall. It must be earned, to begin with, and then it must be responsibly managed. We may be doing the earning now, but our children will most likely inherit both what we have built and the responsibility for its conservation and management. The question is whether or not we can prepare them for that responsibility.

MONEY HAS VALUE

Just as an example of teaching financial responsibility, I'd like to share with you a technique that worked for a family we know well. Many of their friends have tried it with equal success. It's a simple idea.

When their daughter was 12, they decided the best way to teach her the meaning of money was to get her involved with it. They wanted her to be aware of its power and its limitations. The best way to do this, they thought, was to give her a checking account of her own.

Naturally, she was proud and thrilled to have her name on the checks—although understandably the bank was less than pleased. The bankers tried to insist on double signatures, but her parents were determined that she have the full responsibility of spending the money in her account.

Then, after some preliminary window shopping, they worked out exactly what she would need during the coming year, not only for clothes, but also money to cover such necessities as lunch, books, church, records, activities, movies, etc. It was an exercise which required a lot of flexibility on everybody's part, especially, for example, when she insisted on five bathing suits and only two sets of underwear.

But mutual agreement was reached after a democratic discussion and some gentle prodding.

They also included all of her music lessons, school expenses, braces and so forth, divided the figure by 12 and that amount was what her father deposited to her account every month. She thought she'd found the keys to the bank.

There were some problems, of course, but it's out of the problems that the lessons are learned. It wasn't possible at her age to expect her to contribute to the fund, but she was totally responsible for paying her bills on time and managing the money.

When she discovered she would be paying $38 per month on her braces and $32 for her piano lessons, they found her spending a lot more time with her toothbrush and her scales. Her family also won't ever forget her anger and chagrin the time she overdrew her account by 44 cents and the bank sent a debit memo for $3!

The very first November that the plan was in effect, their daughter spent all her clothing money on skirts and sweaters for school. When it occurred to her that she needed a new coat, there was no money for it. She'd made her spending decisions and had to live with the outcome, so she went to school that semester in a coat that was, in her mind, hopelessly out of style (not to mention being a full size too small). She suffered a lot that semester—and so did her mother.

Her father insisted that she couldn't have a new coat until Christmas. She had to manage her money, he said. In retrospect, her mother knows he was right, but at the time it made for some very sporty conversation between her and her husband.

It was also a lesson in quality control. Their daughter found that she could get many more items cheaper at the five and dime—but that economy move reversed itself when everything fell apart after only a few washings. As the years went by, she handled her college tuition, travel, and even her wedding. Today she's a great manager. She learned that the gift of money—like beauty or health—are responsibilities she was privileged to have, not toys to squander or abuse.

It was an excellent learning experience for her and them, and one all involved would recommend to anyone.

But there's more to raising children to wealth than teaching financial responsibility, important though that is. What we are helping prepare our children for is a way of life. That sort of preparation has to be a part of their formative years.

What we, as parents, must accept is that as a result of our efforts our entire family is going to become successful, and we have to handle that fact. Too many men and women have said in their later years—"if only we'd known we were going to be this successful, we'd have raised our children differently."

TEACHING IN THE FORMATIVE YEARS

We must assume that our children will inherit our success, its privileges, and its requirements. Our problem is in finding acceptable models for them to follow—usually a new experience for all concerned.

The major learning period of life takes place in the first 25 years, give or take a few. That's 300 months, which can be divided roughly into three, 100-month periods. Each period is important and each builds on the one that precedes it, but perhaps the most important are the first 100 months.

A child from birth to age eight must be taught four ideals: *Love*, *respect*, *discipline*, and *accommodation*. If we can teach them these concepts, we face much better odds that further essential attitudes and understanding will be developed later.

The *love* a child must learn is not simply love for Mommy and Daddy. It's that, of course, but it's also a love of what his father does. It's a knowledge that Mom loves Dad's work, that Dad loves his work and that both Father and Mother love the life they lead and accept what it requires.

No two, three, or four-year-old child is capable of understanding what his father does, particularly, but he can sense when what his father does makes his mother sad. He can see if Mommy's crying or Daddy's always gone. He doesn't see this as his father's struggle to put bread on the table for all of them. All children see is that whatever their father is doing, it seems to be making their mother miserable, and Dad cranky and tired.

A child may not be consciously aware of what he's feeling—but don't ever doubt that he's feeling. And the bad things that happen in the early months can—and usually do—translate themselves later into an attitude that the business is an evil, destructive influence on all involved. We've heard it too often: "The kids want *nothing* to do with the business."

If we love our businesses, we must make sure we share this love with our children. If we don't love it, what are we doing staying in it?

The lesson of *discipline* is the knowledge that some things have to be done, that they can't be postponed. Discipline means accepting responsibility. Discipline also means that right is right, wrong is wrong. It's a sense of ethics, of propriety, a sense of integrity.

Our business offers us a great life, but our children must see—from our actions—that there are some standards of performance. They must see that things can't always be put off, that benefit follows from contribution.

If Dad is forever talking in front of his heirs about cheating his creditors or fooling the IRS, his example—to the child, becomes what business is all about. A sense of responsibility takes a long time to develop.

This is all learned by example. Children have to start with black and white—they are not experienced enough to evaluate gray.

We have to teach *respect*. Let us control our conversations in front of the young, especially when we are tempted to take pot shots at the dinner table about the transgressions of our employees, our suppliers, or our customers—however tempting it might be after suffering at ther hands. Remember, in 20 years, today's 30-year-old salesman who "drinks too much," is "always" late, "pads his expense account...," may eventually become the 50-year-old vice president of sales and boss of our 25-year-old son who can't wait to get rid of him (and vice-versa).

After 20 years, the supplier, whose quality standards are always discussed negatively, will inevitably be regarded with continuing mistrust and suspicion. After 20 years, customers who always "take advantage" of us are likely to be treated with natural disrespect—with prompt reaction in kind.

It has long been said, "As you sow, so shall you reap."

Finally, heirs must learn *accommodation*, the knowledge that there are other people involved, whose interests, needs, and dreams may rightfully be at variance with theirs. Accommodation is an acceptance of compassion, of understanding, and of trust. It's the opposite of "it's my rattle" or "that's not fair" or "they have more than...."

Very few heirs are only children of only children. Usually, there are brothers, sisters, children of partners, cousins—a whole range of "heirs." *Each must be treated equitably (not necessarily equally)*, and each must understand and accept what is done for and by the other. Accepting this must begin as early as the sharing of toys and duties.

These, then, are our responsibilities as parents—and grandparents—during the first 100 months. If we can teach love, discipline, respect, and accommodation in the early years, we stand a good chance of knowing children of seven or eight who a) think well of business, b) respect what it requires and what it gives to those others who work in varying relationships to us, and c) realize they must blend their requirements to those of their brothers, sisters, cousins and everybody else involved.

The business "lunch" may be ample, delicious and desirable—but it's anything but free.

How we do this for our children differs from parent to parent, from child to child; but if it's not done, then the groundwork has been laid for disaster. If love, discipline, respect, and accommodation are not learned *very early* , the danger increases rapidly that we will have unworthy, imcompetent, irresponsible heirs.

When there's a business involved, money can become a set of loaded, pearl-handled pistols with common stock for bullets. If our heirs are improperly prepared (the terminal disease of too many family businesses), then those fights over the rattle later become fights for "control"—a battle few businesses can afford or survive.

None of us becomes a teacher overnight. Students don't learn overnight. These processes are lifelong pursuits. This is why it's difficult for us to carry out one of our most important jobs as parents—teaching the lessons our children *must* learn early. Nobody has to raise rotten kids. We *can* enter our later years with competent, mature, understanding children. Concentration on teaching the right lessons early is the bedrock for building the future, ours as well as theirs.

THE SECOND 100 MONTHS

This is the time our children should learn the meaning of wealth. This is a major economic lesson and it's best taught before they're sixteen. Sadly, it's on this subject that people are most likely to destroy the character of their children, because they either treat wealth the way Victorians used to treat sex—as something everyone had, but never discussed—or else they take the other extreme and talk about nothing *but* wealth.

We must teach that our money is not evil, that our property and privilege are earned through dedication and hard, honest work. We must show, by example, that our work is a necessary and *enjoyable* part of life, realizing ourselves that work is not something from which our children should be shielded. Learning that our wealth and privileges are earned and not ill-gotten, can do much to make our heirs feel comfortable with what they'll inherit.

A question that comes up again and again at our seminars for young people in family business is "why is it *fair* to have so much when so many others don't?" That's not so different from asking why some people have natural good health, or intelligence, or natural athletic ability. Is that "fair" to those without? Yet, somehow, our children are more comfortable with these gifts than they are with their potential inheritance.

Nobody can control the initial distribution of good fortune. There *is* some luck involved in that. But to enjoy, appreciate and build on what privileges and benefits we're given, we must work. We can be born with health, but we must work to keep it. We can have a chance at education, but we must study to get it. We can inherit wealth, but unless we use it and manage it wisely, it will eventually disappear.

Our children must learn to *respect* what benefits and privileges they have. We must teach them to be comfortable with the family's money without being smug. They must understand what it can do—and what it can't—and how we as parents use it. If they can't manage their own affairs by their mid-teens, what can we expect them to do with the money they'll inherit? Few of us plan on disinheriting our children so they can enjoy the privileges of poverty.

As if financial immaturity were not enough, too many of our children also have a very confused idea about just what their fathers do for a living. Other kids don't seem to have that problem. "My Dad's an electrician/pilot/carpenter/runs a gas station/builds houses..." Other professions seem to be easily identified to children. "My Dad's an English teacher/a lawyer/sells typewriters/works in a bank/writes books..."

Why is it that business owners kids for the most part haven't the foggiest idea what concerns or responsibilities occupy three quarters of their father's waking moments? "My Dad owns his own company" is an unsatisfactory answer because it doesn't explain. As a concept, it's meaningless to children.

As early as possible, in terms and words that will be understandable to their children, fathers and mothers should seek to share the dream of the business—the things it does, the people involved, the markets served, the satisfactions realized, the stories of the past, and the hopes for the future.

How can we expect our children to look forward to a life of commitment to an activity about which they know so little? Let us have them hear from us, their parents, about the joys, the challenges, and the burdens of leadership—of being The Boss and what that really means.

I can guarantee that if we don't, others who have more envy than appreciation will explain to our children what their fathers do, and then we'll have to defend ourselves from *their* criticism.

If we do it right, by the time our children finish their second 100 months, they will have discipline, they will love, they will be able to accommodate others in their family, and they should be comfortable with responsibility. They will have a well-developed respect for money and what it can do, without feeling that the almighty dollar should be their ultimate goal in life.

With this respect, they will be able to take pride in the contribution their family business makes to the world around them.

THE FINAL LESSON: EARNING

This leaves one major lesson. Over the last 100 months of the basic learning period, the years from age 16 to age 25, *our children have to learn their value to themselves and to the world.* The have to learn this realistically. We all want our children to have options, to have comforts, but the way to do this is not to pay a 17-year-old 10 dollars an hour to paint the stripes in the company parking lot. That doesn't teach the economic value of labor and ability. Instead, we should pay them a realistic wage, or, better yet, have them work for somebody else.

Tax advisors can come up with all kinds of tax reasons for overpaying our kids for minimal work under minimal standards, without effective review of accomplishment. But saving on taxes and beating Uncle Sam out of his "undeserved" share, by substituting deductible "wages" for non-deductible "allowance," is no reason to ruin our children. Far better to pay the tax than endorse by our actions a concept of "entitlement" or "deception" as the goal of business ownership.

Children are not born with an understanding of what they can do or what they are worth to others. They surely won't have any idea what to expect of outside employment unless we make sure that they find out. And they'll find it out best in the hands of an objective outsider. Experience has proven it's a good idea to postpone introducing our heirs into the family business until they've had a chance to learn about themselves on their own by encouraging them to get their first jobs from somebody else.

Summer jobs are not the only place to get "outside experience." After they finish their education (the failure to do so can only leave our children less able to compete, with no option left but to "work for the old man"), why don't we encourage our children to use their education, their drive, and their ideas in the marketplace? They could learn valuable management skills which will be so necessary to their successful future responsibilties within their family company.

There are three significant benefits to this. First, it allows the young man or woman the opportunity to collect credentials— by far the most efficient route to gaining credibility in the eyes of non-family employees. Second, working for somebody else can develop a powerful appreciation for the family business. Third, it allows Dad to age a little before his successors agitate for his "retirement."

In the best of all possible worlds, if we do everything right, we will approach our 60's with mature heirs who share our mutual respect and who possess discipline, confidence, experience and even some wisdom. This is what makes retirement an opportunity. We find ourselves teaching while our heirs are happily and competently doing more and more of the work the company will require for *their* success in the future.

Then, if we really want to do some useful work in our golden years, we can help our children teach all these good lessons to *their* little ones...our grandchildren.

"FAIR" DOESN'T MEAN "EQUAL"

We are producing wealth as we build a successful business, and that wealth will, someday, have to be distributed. This will involve some very specific—and often uncomfortable— decisions. The sooner we can foresee the decisions we're going to have to make, the easier it will be for us to do the right thing for our children *and* for the business.

Nancy was facing such questions when I met her. She was the wife of a business owner who was never ready to retire because it wasn't one of his concerns. They founded their music business 15 years ago on "$3000 and a prayer." When her husband died, four years later as the result of a tragic auto accident, Nancy decided to keep the business and run it on her own.

She built a very successful business, and in the process had some very good years. But now she's worried. How can she pass that business on to her children in a way that won't damage or destroy her loving family?

Her most important concern at this point in her life is her children.

"When my husband passed away unexpectedly 11 years ago," she told me, "I was left alone to run the store. Scared and inexperienced, 'Mom' nevertheless had wonderful employees and family. They all pitched in and together we made our business successful, especially George, my youngest son, who has been active in the business for the past 5 years. He's my successor.

"My worry now is how I go about setting up my will—or whatever I have to set up—so that my four children will be treated equally. And, too, I have to do it in such a way that George gets a fair deal."

The "fairness" question, of course, involves her other children, who don't work in the business. The question of how to be fair is probably the most common question wives and widows face.

Nancy has three other children. Gwen is married, but has no children and teaches at a university. Bill is a minister, married, with two children. And Karol, newly married, owns two gift shops with her husband. Their interests just seemed to lie in other directions and, although they each worked part time in the store at one time or another, it never drew them the way it did George. For one thing, he's a semi-professional musician, and music's in his blood.

It seems fairly certain that George is going to run the business after Nancy retires. She is 59 years old. Their two key salesmen, however, are 74 and 69, and not much of a future can be built on them. so Nancy is working hard to turn the management over to George.

But the fact that her other three children aren't going to be involved in the management of the business is causing conflict in her mind about the division of the business. In her words:

"My children *all* want part of the store. We have other property, but it seems to be the store that's the problem. There is a sentimental (and probably financial) attachment which really concerns me, because, while the pressure is there to divide the business four ways, I wonder whether a four-way division is fair to George.

"If I divide it equally, how could he actually ever own the store he's running? What if he started a branch store? Who would own that? I want to treat my children equally, but I worry that somehow this will be unfair to George, that it will put him at a disadvantage.

Nancy is facing a question of differentiating inheritance from opportunity. What she and her husband have built, she'd like to leave to her children, but what George builds should rightly be his. This is Nancy's dilemma, one she's never fully shared with her children.

"Even though my children are all close to one another," she told me, "all married to fine people, they also have a real emotional concern for the store because of their father who started it and their mother who has continued it all these years.

"They all agree that George is the logical one to take over management. Even my two key salesmen are supporting him in every way they can, but I can sense the children are getting touchy about ownership, and I don't want it to destroy our family.

"I guess I've sensed it all along. I've been waiting for something to happen, but I'm the only one who can get the ball rolling to make things happen. All of us—me, the children, their wives and husbands, our advisors, everybody—are going to have to start talking about this. I know most of us are already thinking about it almost full time.

"I may not have the wisdom of Solomon, but I'm beginning to realize that cutting this business in quarters could very well kill the business, and that's the last thing anybody wants."

Many couples who own businesses have a difficult time deciding just how they should divide their estates. They constantly ask: "How can we divide things so that we are as fair as possible to everybody?"

It may help to consider what would happen if we had a mentally or physically "exceptional" child. Surely, neither we nor our other children would object to giving that child special attention or setting aside money to take care of him or her when we are no longer around. What's "fair" would be what meets his or her *needs* .

But in most cases, needs aren't considered when deciding how to distribute an estate. The feeling, instead, is generally that the estate must be divided *equally* , no matter what the consequences, if the division is to be "fair."

A couple I know have shared their estate plans with me, and I feel that they are a good example of people who have defined "fair" according to needs. Fortunately, they have raised their children to trust that their parents will do what is best for everyone. This couple has one son, who is working in the business, and a daughter who is happily married to a very successful attorney in a distant city.

The couple owns all of the property used by the business, and the business rents it from them. The mother's original inclination was to divide this rental income evenly between the two children through the will. Her husband and his advisors convinced her, however, that the last thing their son needed was a distant landlord second-guessing the business decisions he made about the properties.

"We decided that our son should get everything concerned with the business because he has chosen to devote his life to it," she wrote to me, "while our daughter will get our home, possessions and outside investments on the assumption that our son would have first option on the family possessions if she chose to sell.

"This decision was hard for me at first, because I thought we were penalizing our daughter for not being part of the family business. We have discussed all of this thoroughly with both children, and both understand that their inheritances will not be 'equal.' Since they were almost in their teens when we started the business, and saw that we started with nothing, neither has grown up thinking they are going to inherit millions.

"Our son wants the business because he loves it and does a fantastic job. Our daughter's attitude is that whatever she inherits will be more than she expected and she is in total agreement with our decision."

These children understand that the love their parents have for them is expressed in their *not* giving them equal shares of something they would wind up fighting about in the future. And this may be the most precious gift of all.

I feel that we must start early in the lives of our children explaining that "fair" is what Mom and Dad want to do with their estate.

What is *equal*, is our love.

THE IMPORTANCE OF TRUST

Parenthood is no easy job, and there aren't many ways to know for sure whether we're doing that job well. All we can do is our best. Eventually, though, we begin to lose our direct control over our kids, and we find that we have to move, with love, from discipline to *trust*.

When our children are born, we love them so much that we're willing to sacrifice for them. We also force ourselves to discipline them, to teach them right and wrong, so they can grow up to be our pride and joy.

Our experiences with our children weren't unlike yours. When our two-year-old called "come here damn dog," we didn't laugh. We sternly explained that "damn" was not polite. We also made a mental note to see how often it appeared in our own vocabulary.

When one of the local police officers in our small town asked us, again, to tell our youngster to lighten his foot on the gas, we asked the officer to do us a favor, even though it hurt. We asked him to stop our son next time he saw him speeding and give him a ticket.

Of course, there are lots of great memories, too: our teenage daughter coming home from a party at 9:15 because she didn't feel we would approve of what they were serving to drink.

Then there was that phone call one night asking if we were Ty's parents. Our hearts jumped three feet, but it was only an elderly man telling us our son had shoveled his car out of a ditch and wouldn't take anything but a warm "thank you."

These were the days when the kids were home. We still had some control. We could see what they were doing—and what we saw made us proud. We tried to remember to tell them so, too.

But eventually our children leave. They go to college. They get a job out of town. They move into their own place. And almost as inevitably, their lifestyle becomes confusing to us. We get our backs up. We want to issue the edict that "you're our children, and you'll live by our rules."

But we really should ask first whether we've talked about it enough. Have we tried to understand *their* side of the discussion?

We know they don't want to hurt us. Hopefully we've raised them to know what's best for them. Now, we must have the courage to sit down and discuss with them what's bothering us.

For many years, our children lived in our home. We trusted them and they lived up to that trust. If we've trusted them for that long, why should we withdraw that trust because we don't understand?

We've all done the very best job we could when raising our children, and I think it's a safe bet that we all, in fact, *did* a good job. But to act on that bet takes a great act of faith on our part.

Faith has never come easily to anyone, and for people who own businesses, whose children are the key to our future, faith may come even harder. But it must come. Our future will be built on such trust between generations.

Without that, we lose one of the special ingredients that make the family business much more than just another "business."

CXXXXXXXXXD

Chapter 8

Do You Want the Business or Not?

We may be raising great kids, but that doesn't guarantee they're going to have an inbred desire to work with us. In fact, that important decision whether or not to join our family businesses and dedicate their careers to them is one of the hardest our sons and daughters will have to make. Much more is at stake than just a job.

Let me address this chapter to our children, especially those who are uncertain whether or not the family business is for them. My objective is not to sell you on joining the business, but to give you some thoughts on what goes into the decision.

Let's talk about this thing called a career in the family business. Some of you may be wondering why you should choose to come into the business. Your questions may involve just what the business is, and what it is really like working for your parents, usually your father, but also sometimes your mother, your brothers, and your sisters.

What is succession like? What are the problems with gaining credibility? How can both parents and children prepare themselves?

Now, this is by no means a book on succession in the family business. But it *is* a book about how a woman looks at succession, both as a mother, and as someone who has met many young people in the position of having to choose. It's from this point of view that I'd like to say a few words about coming to work for the family business.

While some of you may have rejected the idea of working for your father very early, and others of you may know for sure that the family business *is* your career, for most sons and daughters of business owners, *The Decision* is an ever-present, nagging dilemma.

The key question is not "Should I come into the business?" What you should really be asking yourself is what you want to do with your life. And *that* requires that you think about many more things than just your family business.

A SERIES OF DECISIONS

When and if you decide to work for your family, that choice won't be made in a vacuum. Before making your final choice, you will have to make a whole string of important judgements—whether to make business, itself, your career, for example, as well as how to prepare yourself for that career by gaining the right experience and education. You also will have determined even earlier to find out what business is all about.

To understand if business, or any career for that matter, is worth the further investment of your time, you must *understand* what that career entails. If you don't understand, then you haven't equipped yourself with the facts that are essential to making a sound choice.

Making any decision also implies that you reject many options along the way. You have to choose, for example, not to become a professional athlete, musician, professor, social worker or politician, in order to become a business person.

At one point in your life, these careers and many others like them were possibilities. But as you closed in on your career decision, your range of choices inevitably narrowed.

This should be going on now as you gain in self-knowledge, learn more about your strengths, and develop your interests. With each passing day and each new experience, you should become more sure of yourself and what you want to do.

This is the ideal, anyway. Too often it doesn't go that way.

THE WEALTH OF OPTIONS

The younger you are, in general, the wider your *range* of career options. As you grow older, gain experience and make decisions, you almost certainly eliminate many possibilities, but at the same time you open new choices you didn't have before.

This is why it's so important for you to understand your initial options and where they lead. While we can't predict or control the future, we don't have to make our choices blindly or in a vacuum.

Clearly, some kind of road map to guide you along your career path would help increase your chances of coming out somewhere close to where you want to be.

That road map can be drawn, but *you* have to determine the limits and *you* have to be the designer.

The framework for your plan consists of four very basic questions you will have to ask yourself over and over again as you proceed:

1. *What kind of person am I?*

2. *What do I want out of life?*
3. *How can I keep my necessary options open as long as I need them?*
4. *When must I choose among the options I have?*

To answer the first question, you will have to get to know yourself—something many people fail to do.

Knowing yourself is a difficult process. It takes struggle and often a lot of pain. You have to challenge yourself constantly in order to measure the depth and width of your talents, your abilities, and your limitations. To learn and discover your real strengths and weaknesses, you have to be flexible and willing to try different things.

Ask yourself this question: if you had to tell one story about yourself that would give people an accurate impression of the kind of person you are, what kind of story would you tell?

Would it be about some challenge you met and conquered, or would you tell about what you did on your last vacation? Would you describe your achievements in a hobby you're good at, or would you describe where you live?

You'd probably talk about your challenges, your pursuits and your accomplishments, the things that push you and test you, the activities that help you find out who you are.

This is how you get to know yourself, through the challenges you face on your own: a demanding job, studying for a degree, climbing a mountain, developing a difficult skill. Through these challenges, you will develop the self-knowledge that's the basis for your roadmap.

Deciding on your goals in life will depend a lot on your strengths and weaknesses, your likes and dislikes, the achievements or accomplishments that fulfill you, and what you have found has fleeting value.

The more you know about yourself, the more you will be able to know whether a "goal" you choose really fits you as a person.

For example, if you are a quiet, shy, or reserved person, a job in sales probably wouldn't be best for you. On the other hand, if you are an outgoing person who likes to be with and around people, you would probably want to set goals that would increase your contacts with interesting, vital people. In this case, a job in sales or personnel might be a excellent choice.

Think of your goals in terms of career activity rather than the broader benefits these activities can bring—fame, wealth, security, respect, and the like. In general, the happiest people are those who are working at something they like to do. Once that goal is satisfied, such benefits will follow if they are right for you.

Again this is an ideal. There is no guarantee that life will be either easy or fair, but your chances of having a life you enjoy, life that's happy and productive, are much better if you go after a career that's based on your knowledge of yourself.

Your goals can be many, especially at the outset. You may want to work closely with people, or handle details, or be very active, or travel a lot. Maybe you love doing creative things, spending time in the outdoors, working with electronics or computers.

Explore these interests, asking yourself in what ways you can transfer what you like to do into gainful activities. Every interest can't be turned into a career, of course. That's why people have hobbies. But some can, and should.

Above all, it is important to keep your career options open as long as possible. Options are the cornerstones of any planning you do for the future, but they tend to narrow as time goes on.

For example, your option to be an Olympic gymnast is essentially gone if you haven't started in the sport by the time you're 8. Your option to be a nuclear engineer is generally closed if you did your undergraduate work in French poetry.

Judgements like these are either made early and up front by you—or life will make them for you. Either way, they are made.

If you are going to keep the control of your life in your own hands—as much as any of us can—you must start investing in yourself as intelligently and as soon as possible.

You should invest your time, your effort, your dedication, and your interest in building a personal "resume" that keeps you qualified for the career options you are trying to hold open.

Out of this investment, you will reap such "dividends" as education, skill, experience, credibility, and, above all, confidence in yourself.

You can't prepare for multiple goals indefinitely, but realize that once you stop investing in your qualifications for a given pursuit, you are most likely eliminating that option.

The point is not to hold everything open, but to concentrate wisely.

Eventually, of course, you will have to make some choices. When to do this is probably the most difficult question to decide, and it's the action that's most frequently put off.

Because you can't predict the future, you can never really be *sure* a choice you make will be the right one. All you can hope to know is whether it is right or wrong for you *now*, at the time you make the choice.

If you know yourself, if you've set a good range of reasonable goals you *understand*, and if you've qualified yourself to carry them out if chosen, you will know when it is time to make the important choices.

In other words, you are ready to make choices when you no longer have *major* doubts about your options. Serious questions and doubts are good indicators that you're not ready. They usually have a basis.

Thus, if you decide to choose business as a career over other options, and in conjunction with personal plans such as marriage, children, life style, the choice should come fairly naturally. You should know your strengths and your weaknesses. You should understand the demands business will make. You should have prepared yourself for a business career through education, through experience, or, preferably, both.

You should feel *good* about the decision to go into business. It should follow naturally from what you've done before. And by all means it is a choice you should have made before you make your decision whether or not to come into the family business.

THE FINAL DECISION

Going to work with your family is a serious and major career step. It is *not* like taking a job with General Motors, General Foods, or General Electric. A job with any company other than your own is only that, a job. You can usually move readily from job to job, company to company. Turnover in major corporations is expected and sometimes even encouraged. Experience gained in them is usually easily transferrable.

Such choices don't demand absolute certainty—just a strong desire to make business a career.

But when you join your family's business, you are doing much more than taking a job or just "going into business." You are making a commitment to a joint dream. You are accepting a privilege and a great opportunity in return for which a long-term dedication is rightly expected. Many of the people closest to you will be depending on your actions.

Joining your family's company isn't a casual affair. It's something like a marriage. If you decide later that you made the wrong choice, you can always leave—but not without upheaval and some very hard feelings among the people you love.

Also, experience in a closely-held company, as exciting and challenging as it can be, is not usually transferrable. Experience in these companies is usually highly specialized because the companies themselves are usually highly specialized. The longer you work for your family, the fewer options you will have if someday you decide to leave.

My major advice is to know yourself, your mind, your abilities, and your options .

Then, if you decide to join your family business—one of the most important choices you will ever have to make—you will bring to it the kind of ability and commitment that's absolutely essential.

If you make an plan and follow it, you will most likely make your decision at the right time for all of the right reasons.

I'd like to give you some "Rules of Career Planning" which were put together a few years ago by Donald Jonovic, vice president of our Center for Family Business. They sum up very well what I've said above.

SOME RULES OF CAREER PLANNING

1. What you deeply desire today will seem a little foolish tomorrow.

2. You will change.

3. All men may be created equal, but life has a way of changing all that.

4. You will someday wish you'd listened.

5. Older people know much less than they think...

6. ...and a lot more than you think.

7. You will never have all the facts.

8. Procrastination is best put off until later.

ひXXXXXXXXXひ

Chapter 9

Is There Love after Succession?

Since the best way to understand a way of life is usually to talk to those who live it, it seems appropriate, at this point, to hear from children of business owners who have gone through, or are going through, the painful process of management succession in a family business.

Let me present the thoughts of three successors whom I came to know very well. Each comes from a different perspective and has a viewpoint based on different experiences, but I think you'll be surprised how well they supplement each other.

STARTING AT THE BOTTOM

Today, Steve is the vice-president of his family's publishing firm. He's 33 and has been working in the business for 12 years, very successfully. Steve talks easily about his college days—which he believes he mostly wasted—and his first, learning years in the business.

"My Dad started the business in 1958, just when he turned 50. He'd worked for an educational publishing company for 25 years and had planned on buying that company, but all kinds of problems developed. He decided, instead of fighting it, to start out on his own.

"I remember he came home from work one day when I was 12 and told us he'd quit and was starting up a new company. That same afternoon he went out and bought cameras, presses, desks, chairs and rented some space.

"The next day he was in business.

"I first worked in the business during my first summer home from college. I didn't have a job and my Dad suggested that if I wanted to, I could go down to the plant and work for the summer. You know, the whole idea scared me to death. I didn't want to be the boss's son and all the problems that go along with it.

"But, obviously, I did it. I started working, and, of course, all I did were very menial jobs. I swept around machines. I did everything I could to just stay by myself back in the shadows.

"Well, that's not quite true. I did strike up a few relationships with people I liked, but I really didn't learn much about the business. I was watching the machinery, which, in our business is fun to watch, and this is probably what gave me my first inkling that there was something I liked about the company. It's a *tenseness* in the air that keeps you alert, watching what's going on.

"So at the end of that summer, my Dad and I had a talk and I told him I might like to try it again."

Steve was in college at the time, in business administration, but he doesn't feel he owes much of his success to his education.

"It was the old story. I never had to study very hard in high school, so in college I was on probation with something like a 1.3 average. I had a good time, sure, but I really didn't have much self-confidence. I was beginning to worry that I was really dumb. I couldn't even transfer because my grades were so low.

"I played pool all the time. I cut classes. Probably six hours a day, five days a week, I played pool. As I got more sure I'd be going into the family business, I relaxed more on studying. I didn't *have* to get good grades."

But then Steve had an experience which underlines the advice we give to young people trying to decide what to study in school—take subjects you like, from teachers who love their subjects.

"Then something positive happened. I found something to be interested in. I started taking English courses and really liking them—in one class, I was the only non-English major, and the only one getting an A.

"I got involved with theater and I started writing short stories and plays. You should've seen me. I looked like a pool shark and I was hanging around with all the longhairs at the theater. But my confidence went up and, in my last semester, when I desperately needed three A's to graduate, I got them all. I got two 95's and a 97 on my finals.

"That convinced me that I could do what I had to do if I wanted to do it bad enough."

Steve worked every summer during college and then started full time after graduation. His developing confidence was showing in his work during the summers, and he'd moved up every year.

While working all day, he never saw his Dad. But as his father saw his increasing interest, they spent many a night at the dining room table after dinner, planning machinery moves, and improving shop procedures. They really got so they enjoyed each other's company and respected the other's opinion.

"When I came with the company, one of the things I made my Dad promise was that I would never get a raise or promotion on his say so. It would have to come from one of the department heads when they believed I deserved it.

"Then, that year, just a few months after I started, my Dad had his heart attack and I found out, at 22, that nobody in the company knew how to work with writers, nobody knew how to do billing, work with the bank, you name it...and that included me. Dad had been doing all that himself.

"Dad had the attack on a Monday. On Tuesday, I had a meeting with all the department heads and told them what had happened. I said there was no way I was qualified to give final approval to important or tricky jobs. I said I'd help with priorities, stuff like that.

"Needless to say, that didn't work, I was the owner's son. I was the boss and I had to take the responsibilities. No one else would—Dad had never let them.

"I grew up real fast."

Today, 12 years later, Steve is married and the father of two children. His Dad is "almost" fully retired, and Steve has every right to his confidence. He earned it the hard way, with customers and employees.

His Dad still worries that his son will forget to do something important, but Steve's a good son and keeps his Dad informed. To help his wife understand the tremendous demands the business puts on his him, they've both become very active in a local association of young executives in family businesses. She's proud of him and what he's done. He's done a good job of sharing the dream, of growing up in the business from the bottom up.

STARTING NEAR THE TOP

Ken, who has been president of his family company for more than three years is able to look at succession from the point of view of someone who is no longer a successor. He's been chief executive officer of his business since his dad died.

"I've always been an outgoing guy—some people would probably call it aggressive—but I'll tell you that walking into my Dad's business as the heir-apparent was one of the hardest things I ever did.

"I think it has something to do with how people think about wealth. They have this idea that if something's not *earned*, it's unjust or immoral, or worse. That leaves a lot of room for guilt in those who get something for nothing.

"When I was a young naval officer right out of college, I was put in charge of men, some of whom had much the same background I did—the same education, everything. But I had the bars. I was the boss.

"I could have been friends with some of the sailors in my division, but it was impossible. There was an invisible shield between us called 'gold braid' and the whole system was set up to keep that shield there. At least in the Navy there were other officers. You weren't alone.

"When I came into the business, however, it was more like my days as a midshipman on summer training cruises. Then I was working with the crew, but had to wear this silly hat with a blue stripe. Everyone knew damn well who I was and what I was going to be someday—their boss.

"That's how I felt joining Dad's business as 'The Kid.'

"I was 25, fresh out of the Navy with an unused—but real—engineering degree in my hand. I even had that degree on the wall in my office for a while until I realized it wasn't doing me any good up there.

"I learned the same lesson in the Navy when I found out that being called an 'ensign' didn't make you an officer. You can get rank and title, but that's no guarantee of respect. I only became an officer the day my subordinates, the petty officers, determined among themselves that I probably wouldn't screw things up too much if left to my own devices—and even then, I only became *effective* once they respected my opinion.

"In the business, I tried hiding behind my degree, until I realized the only person impressed by it was me.

"It wasn't that the draftsmen in the shop rejected me or undercut me or anything like that, but it was my *father* they respected. He was the one who'd hired them. He made the decisions. I was just The Kid, a fact I couldn't change by wishing it away.

"So I decided that if I worked twice as hard as everyone else, nobody could throw too many rocks at me. I figured that getting all hung up on whether other people respected me wouldn't solve anything. I respected myself and had confidence in myself, so I decided that their respect would come or not come as they saw fit—and as I built up a track record on the job.

"Maybe I should've started out somewhere else. I know a lot of guys do, but there was no question of my doing that. First of all, we didn't have the time to do it. My dad was 62 when I joined the business and not in the best of health. Second, I was a graduate engineer with more technical training than most of the men on the staff. And, third, I wasn't about to start at the bottom. As I said, I'm an aggressive guy—and I had ideas.

"Starting out with some responsibility from the beginning wasn't really new to me. I had to do that in the Navy. Besides, I knew only one thing really mattered when it came to getting respect from the people who work for you: you have to be *good*.

"I made it a point to be better than anybody else in the company at what I was doing—which, in the beginning, was sales. I tried to look at the job as though I was working for somebody else, not my father, and if I didn't work out, I'd be out in the street.

"That wasn't actually true. I was Dad's only hope. If I didn't work out, he was planning on selling to the employees—which wouldn't have worked, either—or just folding up, which would have left a lot of guys out on the street. You see, we're basically a service business, with not much to sell but a name and reputation. If I couldn't hack it, there wouldn't have been a business.

"I was realistic. I got the vice-presidency of the company over a lot of other capable, more 'experienced guys,' simply because my name was the same as the owner's. I knew if I let that go to my head, I was through. I'd never be worth much.

"I suppose I felt my advantage was a little unfair. But I'm not really a guy to sit around and worry about things. The chance was there, I wanted to be president, so I plunged right in.

I asked Ken what this meant to his wife and his young family. He said that early in the game he decided he could only fight one war—out on the streets, not in the house. He didn't have energy enough to do both. The demands of the job, and the price of failure would be so great that he decided he'd best make an ally out of his wife so she could realize it was for *them* he was doing it.

"In the beginning, I had some trouble with the employees—but I expected that and lived with it as best I could. I knew as soon as I started bringing in new jobs the chill would disappear. After all, these guys weren't blind and they could see my Dad couldn't last forever. And there was no way they could afford to buy him out.

"They may have resented me, but I was really their best bet for keeping their jobs.

"Well, to be perfectly modest, it turned out that I was pretty good—and not only at sales. I made it a point to get to know as much as I could about everything going on in the company and I was able to earn a few medals as a manager, too.

"The most important ingredient in getting credibility out of the older employees, I think, is always doing your homework and making sure you are better than anyone else at your job.

"You know, as I listen to myself, I begin to sound like a hero, but that's because I never mentioned all the times I screwed up. I said I thought about the early days a lot—and I do. Mostly, I'm embarrassed.

"Besides, heroes are made not born, and a little selective amnesia never hurts the image."

MAKING IT AS A DAUGHTER

Finally, I'd like to introduce you to a very unusual person, a daughter/successor. Tricia is 24, an only child, and currently vice president of her family's construction machine distributorship in the midwest. She often drives herself in a 20-foot truck to haul bulky demonstration machines to potential customers, and she is one of very few women in the country doing this.

Even though she was hired in sales by her father because he reasoned that she'd be less embarrassed failing for him than somebody else, she is now accepted by him and her industry as a knowledgeable, capable salesperson.

Tricia told us that her Dad really didn't expect her to make it in sales—particularly selling machinery, and she believes that much of that opinion was based on the fact that she was his daughter and, therefore, female.

"My Dad is extremely chauvinistic. That's not a fault—it's a characteristic. He was amused the first three months I was making sales, really amused, but after a while he began to think maybe we had something here. His attitude changed.

"I had to prove to him, though, that this was more than just a lark. He even said to my mother once that he gave me six months, *max*. He figured I'd hit a bad string of construction sites and that would be it.

"I think fathers tend to be harder on daughters."

Of course, an opposite point could be made. We could expect that, because fathers and daughters are traditionally closer than fathers and sons, fathers should be gentler with their daughters. Tricia doesn't think that closeness necessarily works in the daughter's favor, however.

"Fathers assume a male can take on certain responsibilities, but they don't make that same assumption about their daughters. Somehow they think femininity makes you less able to work in a man's world.

"Therefore, a daughter has to work three times as hard to prove she's willing, three times as hard to prove she's capable. My Dad just doesn't want to think of me as a woman out on a job site in galoshes and everything. He wants to think of me in a pink dress, sipping tea.

"I will never be one bit less his little girl, no matter how much I sell or how many job sites I visit, I'll never lose that image. I'll always be Daddy's little girl.

"Sons don't have to jump that identity hurdle. I think all a son has to do is indicate that he may be just a little bit interested and all kinds of responsibility is given to him—almost automatically.

"His father may be critical later of what the son does with the responsibility, but he gives it to him readily."

Tricia, of course, has crossed that initial barrier. Now the question arises whether there are differences between the ways daughters and sons work with their fathers. One major difference from Tricia's point of view, is that she doesn't think daughters feel a sense of competition with their fathers—or vice versa.

ARE DAUGHTER/SUCCESSORS DIFFERENT?

"There is a much stronger emotional tie between a father and a daughter than between a father and a son. Sons want more to be like their fathers, and often they think they have to be better. I know of one situation, for example, where father and son race the clock every morning to get in earlier than the other.

"Fathers and sons tend to move toward equal status—at least that's what the sons are looking for. That's competition. But I don't picture myself on the same level with my father, and I'm not in competition with him because I could never surpass what he's done.

"Competition doesn't seem to be an issue between my father and me, not the way it would probably be if I were his son."

But that doesn't mean she doesn't expect problems in the future.

"My biggest challenge will be in having him accept my decisions. The most difficult thing for him will be learning to trust my busness judgment. I think it's easier for a man to trust another man.

"Then, too, there's the problem of my future husband, whoever he may turn out to be. We haven't really discussed it, but I'd say Dad's thinking that he'd like the man I marry to get involved with the company, and eventually run it. I don't think it's occurred to him that maybe my husband won't want to run the business, that he'll have his own career totally.

"I'd even be happy if my husband decided to join us and became the president over me. I'd be very pleased with that. Although I wouldn't have the total responsibility, I could still have a decision-making role because of my experience in sales.

"Working in a family-owned company isn't a job. It's a way of life. Like it or not, that's the way it is. You live and breathe the business. It's always in the back of your mind. I would never be cut out of it.

"But as much as I'd be comfortable with my husband becoming my Dad's successor, I still think it's possible for a woman to be a chief executive and have a family at the same time. You have to have very good managers and you have to delegate a lot, but it can be done.

"My job has been a great thing for both my Dad and me. I see more of him than I've ever seen. I can appreciate his business sense and his ability. We're even closer than we were when I started working for him, something that might not have happened if I were his son.

"I've seen a lot of sons and fathers ending up on opposite poles in a very short period. There's a lot more electricity in the air in those situations, because of that competitiveness we talked about.

"Maybe the sons push harder and fathers are always reluctant to give up power. Maybe they're too much alike. I'm not sure. But I *do* know my Dad and I have a lot more relaxed relationship than most sons and fathers, and I like it that way."

Listening to these youngsters makes it all seem worthwhile. As we get older, it seems so easy to find flaws in our propects for the future, but I'm sure you'll agree—children who share our dream are our hope for tommorrow.

CRRRRRRRRRS

Chapter 10

So You're Marrying the Boss's Kid

You've just gotten engaged to a wonderful person. His or her father owns a great family business and your future spouse will be an heir to that business, possibly even the successor. That makes you a potential successor's spouse...and a potential spouse of a business owner.

It's a wonderful life, and you have my congratulations. But before you begin, I'd like to share with you some ideas people who've succeeded in this role have shared with me.

If your wife-to-be is the daughter of a business owner, she might be a successor, but statistics stand against that probability. If she is, of course, everything said about marrying successors will hold in your case, with the additional wrinkle that fathers don't compete with their daughters. They're more likely not to take them seriously. This is a problem you will have to live through and overcome together.

Even if your future wife won't be working for her father, you will probably find that her brother or brothers do. You may even find yourself invited to join the company—particularly if there are no sons interested or old enough. If you decide to join your father-in-law in business, you will then have that exciting experience reserved for successors to business owners, in addition to fighting Dad's vague conviction that somehow his baby could've done better in choosing a husband.

But let me concentrate on another problem I feel more qualified to discuss—the problem of being the *wife* of a business owner's heir.

First of all, you must be prepared to accept the fact that those who own their own businesses get passionately attached to the all-consuming goal of making them successful. They enjoy the challenge and accept the demands those businesses make on both their time and their energy.

This is something you must try to understand, and you must not allow it to make you feel neglected and resentful. I know of no public corporation that can give you more freedom, both economic and physical, than the family-owned company, and I believe the sacrifices are worth the results.

Secondly, the standard requirement that you be supportive of your spouse becomes even more important when a family business is involved—especially if your spouse is a *son* of the owner. It's difficult to follow in the footsteps of a successful father, and a young man's identity often gets confused. Is he Tom Smith, or the *son* of *Bob* Smith?

A successor needs support and encouragement. He must go out and prove to himself, for his own confidence and to gain the respect of others, and to do that he needs your help.

Finally, it's very likely that your father-in-law is a dynamic, high-powered, take-charge man. This situation has a tendency to emphasize the successor's subsidiary role and this, in turn, is likely to amplify your natural, loving desire to make sure your husband is appreciated. What you have to avoid is allowing your "mother tiger" instinct to take over.

ENCOURAGEMENT, NOT AGGRESSION

I would suggest that you encourage your husband to be assertive in his own way and in his own time. Your own instincts may unwittingly come out in the company of others and this can make him come out to seem *less* than he is rather than more. Any aggressiveness on your part should be expressed to him, in private, because otherwise, instead of helping him, you could destroy what you would like to build.

You face a number of jobs. You must encourage your husband to be assertive. You are needed to support him in his struggle to find his place, and you must understand the massive demands a family-owned business can make on both of you.

Believe me, I fully understand your difficulties. Among the letters I've received was one from a very confused daughter-in-law, who had recently married into a family that owned a business.

She married into a "great" family, to use her word, one in which everybody enjoys each other. She's fully accepted by her parents-in-law.

But she has a problem. Every time she has some "constructive" criticism, or a comment about the business, her in-laws make her feel that she's stepping out of bounds.

"It's not so much that they *tell* me to mind my own business," she wrote, "as it is the way they either smile tolerantly at my suggestion, or pounce on it as superficial or plain wrong, or just pretend I never said it."

This hurts her, she said, and she wonders why she seems to be treated as an outsider when she's supposed to be part of the family.

HOW DO THEY SEE THE BUSINESS?

It's important in this kind of situation for the daughter-in-law to understand the relationship that exists between her "in-laws" and their business. For them, particularly if they founded the business, there's a strong emotional tie to the company—almost as though it were one of their children.

This is a very special "child," and its "parents" are almost naturally overprotective. They resent any criticisms or suggestions as indications that their beautiful offspring is somehow less than it should be.

(Maybe I should change "it" to "she," because this special child is really similar to a little girl who was always "protected.")

This might not be the healthiest reaction they could have, but it's very real and honestly felt. Their intent is not to exclude the daughter-in-law, so much as it is to shield this business "child."

It might very well be that the daughter-in-law, as someone who was not raised in the business, can see things that the family cannot see because they are too emotionally involved. Her opinions could even be valid. But valid or not, they will have no impact at all unless they are accepted.

This is why it's helpful to think of the business as another "child." Few of us are likely to jump right in and criticize someone's children, because we all recognize, almost automatically, that such things must be done sensitively, carefully, and with understanding.

I'd suggest to this young woman that she go very slowly. Take the time to learn, asking them, for example, to explain the business—both how it started and what their dreams for it are.

She should also discuss her thoughts with her husband, because he will have a good idea how his family will react to her suggestions. He can also help bridge the gap, and help her help them understand that she's not a threat to their "special child."

Most of all, they need time to understand and know that she really does care. It can't be forced, and it must be done slowly.

THE DISHONESTY OF HONESTY

At one of our recent seminars, I spent a lot of time with a group of young people who prided themselves on being "completely honest." They told me, however, that they were having difficulty because other people were misinterpreting their intent and resenting what they said.

We talked about why such a very fine trait as honesty could cause so much pain, and I found the following example was very helpful to our discussion.

I know of a very fine clergyman who once gave a sermon on "honesty" and "being true to one's self." His audience listened closely, maybe too closely, because the effect of his sermon was not at all what he expected.

It didn't take long for discord to build up among some members of his congregation, and it wasn't too many Sundays before he was forced to give another sermon entitled "Honesty Needs Compassion."

Because he'd encouraged so much "honesty," hard feelings were developing within his flock. For example, one lady member of the congregation had purchased a new dress to wear to a charity benefit. She made the mistake of seeking the opinion of an acquaintance who had listened carefully to the minister's sermon.

"Don't you love my dress?" she asked. "I've always wanted a chance to wear this style."

The reply she received was nothing if not honest: "Not really. That style isn't very flattering to you."

Then there was also a young couple showing off their new baby, who had asked, "Isn't he just beautiful?"

The reply they received was also very honest: "He's really very sweet, but I wouldn't say he was beautiful."

What good did honesty do for these people?

Since the woman was obviously enjoying wearing her new dress, what harm would there have been in answering her question with something like: "It's a striking style, and the color looks great on you." Although this doesn't directly answer the question, neither does it compromise honesty or hurt her feelings.

And as for the baby, couldn't we remember how wonderful it is that God allows each parent to see their own baby as the most beautiful child in the world?

We discussed these questions and others at that seminar, and came to three conclusions:

First, honesty is not something to hide behind so it will be easier to "express" ourselves.

Second, "honesty" is no excuse for poor manners.

Third, tempering our honesty with compassion not a compromise of that honesty. It's a way to save a lot of unnecessary heartache.

In short, if we care about the feelings of others, honesty, compassion, and tact must all be used *together*.

In the family business, as in all human relationships, too much "honesty" can, and often does, create a problem. The fragile and valuable relationships we share require that we blunt the sharp cutting edge of truth.

When honesty is tempered with compassion, it shows that we care. And this, if you are going to marry the boss's son, is the most important thing you can show your new family.

BROTHERS AND SISTERS—IN LAW

There's another problem you should be aware of as a potential business owner's daughter-in-law. Few bosses have only children. You may have only one husband, but there are usually other offspring within the family who have as much an interest in the business as you do.

Why is this a problem? Mostly because only one of the successors can be president. This can be a very hard truth for the spouses of those who aren't selected. Marie is such a person. I met her a couple of years ago, just after a new president was elected in her husband's family business. Because of the way the announcement was handled, and because Marie wasn't prepared to accept the news, that business found itself in a whole lot of trouble.

"Dad just announced it at Thanksgiving dinner," Marie told me. "He said he was going to make Harry president after January 1st and Mike only vice president.

"I think it's an insult. Mike's his son, and Harry's only his son-in-law..."

These were Marie's exact words, including the "onlies," which themselves tell a lot about what she was thinking.

Marie and her husband were 28 at the time. Harry, the son-in-law chosen for the president's job was 36. Marie just couldn't see any reason why Harry should have been president "just because he was older."

"Mike's every bit as good as Harry," she complained to me. "After all, they're both paid the same. I just think Dad should have thought of his son ahead of anybody else."

Marie's husband had joined his father's business five years before, while Harry had been working with the company since he married Bonnie, about 13 years. Marie recognized the longer tenure Harry had, but thought that wasn't so important since Harry "didn't even have an MBA."

Marie was upset. That was obvious. It was clear there was a major problem brewing which her father-in-law was going to have to solve. The fact was, though, it needn't have happened in the first place.

I asked Marie what her husband thought about the choice of Harry as president.

"He hasn't said much, really," she told me. "He and Harry have always been the best of friends, and they work well together, so he seems to figure it's best not to say anything. But I know he's hurt. Wouldn't you be?"

A few days later, I had a chance to talk to Mike, himself, to get his thoughts about being "passed over" as president of his father's company. I congratulated him on his promotion to vice president and he thanked me—but I could see he wasn't thrilled. I told him so.

"No," he protested. "I really am, I guess. I mean it's probably the right thing for Dad to do. But I've got to admit I really got upset. When he first said it, I was fine, but later as I thought about it, it really started working on me.

"It's got nothing to do with Harry, you know. He's a great guy, and very capable. It's not that. I just always somehow thought that I ... Well, it's *our* business and ... well, I thought I'd be president."

When I asked Mike if he'd talked this over with his Dad, he told me he hadn't, that there was no reason to. Mike believed his father had made up his mind and that was that.

If ever an important decision wasn't accepted in a family business, it was this one. A wound was opened and, although it wasn't being talked about, it showed all the signs of getting ready for a long fester.

I mention this situation, because the problem is so common. If we are going to survive as family businesses we have to be able to sit back and look at what is happening to us from some perspective. The experiences of others can help us.

There are some important questions to ask here. For example, was the real problem the promotion of the son-in-law, the way it was handled, or something else entirely? What could the father have done to guard against this result? How could his wife have helped in gaining acceptance? What should he have done once the announcement was made?

ONLY ONE CAN BE PRESIDENT

A basic fact that everybody involved with a successful family-owned business must acknowledge is that there can only be one president. When there is only one heir and successor, this fact is readily embraced by everybody. But single successors are in the minority, and problems can occur in families with multiple heirs, particularly bitterness and disappointment, which can tear their businesses apart.

There's no universal law of family business that says once the next president is chosen, everybody else interested in the job should bail out. People should be able to work together in a hierarchy.

But gaining the necessary cooperation is a big job, a continuing job, that begins the day potential successors express interest in the business.

All sorts of "creative" solutions to this problem keep coming up from all kinds of people. One such idea is the "rotating presidency." For example, this question was recently asked at one of our seminars: "With four sons in the business, it is now our plan that every seven years we elect a new president, and that the outgoing president will become chairman of the board. Assuming all four sons are competent, are there any real flaws in this plan?"

Rotating presidencies are almost universally disasters. Plans which sound good on paper or in theory always have to face people—real people. In the questioner's business, for example, the family would have to go through a 21-year period in which there will be chaos as the retired older sons second-guess the younger son, and all of them tower over the fourth son who not only had to wait 21 years to take over, but now has three effectively "retired" past presidents on his board.

We can't rotate talents and abilities like crops, and we can validly question the assumption that all four sons are "competent." After all, who judged them? Mother? Father? Their wives?

Even if they are competent, they won't necessarily each have all the right abilities at exactly the right times.

Other such ideas have included the "co-presidency," which makes agreement mandatory on all matters (a very difficult thing to do), or using a "family council" to help decide all the tough (and sometimes even the not-so-tough) matters— where everybody has a vote, by blood, by marriage, and by right (by darn!).

But the fact is that some decisions simply cannot be abdicated. Succession must be decided on as early as practicable—and this was done in Mike and Harry's case. Once it's decided by those whose responsibility it is to do so, everybody involved must be brought in on the decision so they can learn to agree from the beginning. This Dad and Mom failed to do.

SEPARATING FAMILY FROM BUSINESS

There is another very real and serious problem you will probably face if you marry into a family business. To live and thrive in this kind of environment, you will sooner or later have to learn how to separate family concerns from business concerns.

A few years ago, I met Beverly, a business owner's daughter. Beverly's husband, Steve, worked with her father and was the designated successor. Like any boss/successor combination, the two men often had disagreements, and had just disagreed strongly the week before we met. The disagreement went on for several days. Although each man respected the other, neither would give in.

Beverly wasn't sure what the disagreement had been about, but that wasn't even important. What was bothering her was the way Steve responded to the problem.

She, quite innocently, had invited her parents over for dinner that weekend. Even though she knew nothing about the problem Steve and her father were having, Steve felt her inviting them over for dinner meant she had sided against him.

Steve, of course, wasn't the president of the company, and he realized that his idea would probably be tabled. He was frustrated and very angry. When his in-laws came to the house that weekend, he could hardly hide the frost in his attitude. It was a totally miserable time for him, and even worse for Beverly.

Even more exasperating for Steve was the fact that his father-in-law acted as though there were no harsh feelings at all between them that preceeding week.

Needless to say, after Beverly's parents left that night, the young couple got into a long "discussion."

Beverly was as bewildered by Steve's attitude as he was by hers. In her family, a very specific point was made to separate family dinners from family *business* dinners. Ever since she could remember, the rule had been that the family discussed business, argued and compromised, only when they gathered together specifically to do that. If they were getting together socially, however, all business feeling had to be put aside.

Like so many families with years of experience working together in a business, Beverly's family realized if this wasn't done, the family would spend all their time together haggling over business.

As important as the company was to them, they realized there was much more to family life than that. They also realized how explosive business discussions could become. Constant disagreement about business matters was not only bad for the two couples, it was completely unfair to the grandchildren.

But Steve hadn't been brought up in this environment. It didn't occur to him that business and family had to be separated at times. Beverly didn't understand his attitude. He didn't understand why she didn't understand this. No wonder they were confused.

Once Beverly and I had a chance to talk, she began to see what was happening, and realized she and Steve were going to have to come to the same agreement to separate their family life and their business life. I'm happy to say, from what I've heard, they were able to do it.

Marrying the boss's kid can be the first step into a great future, but, as I hope you can now see, you have to keep careful watch on where you step—and how.

You are about to embark on what I consider to be a most exciting life, the life of a member of a family owning a business.

If you choose to stand on the outside looking in, you will find yourself in the position of an outsider. If you are willing to make the effort to understand the joys as well as the demands the family business makes, you will find it presents a challenge and a source of satisfaction.

CXXXXXXXXXXD

Chapter 11

Enter Our Son's New Bride

We all have the opportunity of raising our own children to believe and respect what we believe and respect. Often we even succeed.

But there are also many other people who join our family from the outside, people who've been raised by others. We don't know them. They don't know us. They're our *instant family* : sons-in-law, partners, partners' wives and kids, and, probably most important—though usually neglected, if not ignored—our daughters-in-law.

We have to expend the same care and interest on our instant family as we do on our regular family, only we have to do it a lot smarter and a lot faster. Their influence on the future of the business is great and will grow greater as time goes by.

Consider the daughter-in-law. This woman will have an influence over her husband—our son—which is increasingly more powerful and more pervasive than any his parents could hope to have. When she joins the family, she's an outsider. She's uncomfortable about her role and her husband's work. If we neglect her, she often has little option other than to become a determined enemy. She will fight to defend and support only what she loves and understands.

Obviously, we can't control the destiny of our children by picking out their mates. Those days are gone, thank goodness. What we *can* do is raise our own children well and pray a lot that their spouses will try to understand us and our value system. They have to accept us and what we do in our sense of fairness, as we have to accept them.

This doesn't happen automatically. As soon as that lovely young woman crosses her new threshold, maybe even before, we must bring her into the family and explain with love what we are doing, why we are doing it, and who seems to fit where. She must really feel that she is welcome and that her concerns are always going to be important to us.

Too often, these feelings aren't shared. We must remember, our son picked this woman because he loved her, and we must try to accept her as our own.

LOVING THE SAME MAN

Over and above her problem adjusting to the demands of a business that's new to her, in addition to the family's initial discomfort with this "outsider," I believe that mothers and daughters-in-law frequently have trouble getting along. This is primarily because they love the same man, and fail to realize that their loves are not competitive. Instead of seeing the good they can do together, mothers and daughters-in-law too often tend to compete.

Mom thinks she's threatened. She's also a little jealous—probably mostly unconsciously—because she wonders how this comparative stranger can understand her son's real needs as well as she.

For her part, the daughter-in-law is too often fearful of the closeness she feels between her husband and his mother, because she thinks it will get in the way of "independence" for her in her own new family.

These fears are usually unfounded, but because they are believed, and consequently acted upon, the worst usually happens.

Instead of competing, what Mom and her daughter-in-law need to do is understand how their places in the family actually *complement* each other.

Mom must remember that she has raised her son to be independent—one of the best gifts a parent can give—and if his independence didn't destroy his love for her before, it won't now that he's married.

Love can be expressed in many ways, and it's inevitable that her son's expressions will change as his family grows. But Mom should look forward to the joy that can come from a proud son who shares with his children his love for his own parents. Being a grandparent is one of God's greatest gifts. We just have to be wise enough to enjoy it.

The daughter-in-law, in return, has to understand that there's no "competition" for the kind of love that exists between husband and wife. This love is a love composed of commitment and sharing, the kind of love every married couple needs to help face the future with confidence.

If these ideas are understood by Mom and her daughter-in-law, it will help eliminate many of the stresses so common in the life of a family business. Sons of business owners have enough pressure on them without having to be caught in the middle of a feud between the most important women in their lives.

There's no way to be practical when it comes to love, but we can perhaps be wise. I remember what my grandmother used to say about love:

"Don't be afraid to give your love away," she told me so many times, "because when you do, it will grow and come back to you in even greater measure."

I've always taken this to mean that love cannot survive when it is held too close to the heart. One of the surest ways to stifle love is to resent love when it is expressed to others.

The "in-law gap" can only be bridged when such understanding exists on both sides. Both mother and daughter-in-law must realize that neither will be threatened by the other as long as both can learn to accept their mutual love for the same man.

WHEN SONS ARE FORCED TO CHOOSE

Making sure our sons' wives are on our side is no mere exercise in family public relations. Remember that her last word every night goes a long way towards guaranteeing, or destroying, our carefully laid plans—for succession and everything else.

There's a manufacturing firm on the East Coast, for example, founded and built by a very competent engineer. There are three sons, all married. At 41, the oldest—and by far the most capable—had long been considered his father's choice for the presidency, because the other two boys, who were both much younger, were also far both less motivated and less qualified.

The oldest son has just recently announced, however, that he's leaving the family company to start his own business, mostly because the wife he loves is just not comfortable with his family. She's a fine person, a good wife, but she'd always felt left out of those family decisions that involved her future.

She's a nurse—capable, hard working, and well-respected in her profession. But her father-in-law had always believed a wife's place was in the home, and because of that she thought he had never accepted her. He seldom talked to her and she always resented the great power he had over her husband and her life. The truth is, her father-in-law was shy, but she had no way of knowing that.

It's become a no-win situation. This fine family business is going to suffer because of inattention to the need to make this young woman understand and participate in the hopes for the future.

There are cases, of course, where there's little hope of success in the marriage from the beginning.

Young men have been known to exercise colossally bad judgment in picking a mate. Sons in their mid-twenties have been known to go off and marry 45-year-old divorcees with children from three previous marriages; or daughters have married adventurers who expected the business to support their indulgences on the pain of divorce or the threat of never being able to see the grandchildren.

Even on such simple things as location and lifestyle, some marriages can foreshadow problems in planning for a business's future.

These things have happened before. They'll happen again.

Still, in most cases, our sons will marry wonderful women. We have to work hard, with candor, openness, and love, however, to bring that new family member into our house and our hearts, and we have to begin without delay.

There are many ways this can be done. Some families schedule family meetings devoted to the progress of the business and discussions of plans for the future. Others simply make sure that the wives of both involved and uninvolved sons are kept informed, and treated so that these women know that their thoughts are valued.

What is important in every case, however, is that Dad feel comfortable with his son's wife, and just "talk" to her about the business and the family. Mom could spend some time doing this too. This new member of the family will have questions, many of them, but they won't be asked unless they're encouraged. The answers have to be honest ones—she's wagering a lot on her husband's happiness and success in the business.

It won't work just to say, "I can't stand her, so there's no point in talking." Once our son has made his choice of mates, we are only making a foolish mistake forcing him to choose between us and the young woman he married. The cards are stacked in *her* favor.

If the channels of discussion are opened early and constantly, she can become one of the most effective guarantees of the continuity of the business, with its hopes and dreams for all.

Perhaps it would be helpful if we could hear from a successor's wife who didn't feel included.

A DAUGHTER-IN-LAW SPEAKS

Elizabeth is the wife of a successor to a family business, who, when she got married, entered a world totally new to her. She had no experience with family business—her father had a minor managerial job for a large public company—so she looks at her role and the family business from the point of view of an outsider. But she is thoughtful and articulate, however, and she presents an intelligent, sensitive view of a daughter-in-law's world as she sees it.

In many ways, she also seems to present a militant view. She shows many hard, sharp edges. In her attitude, Elizabeth is like many successors' wives we've met over the years. It's not that she's combative by nature. Instead, she feels she's being kind of backed into a corner. She thinks she understands, but doesn't think she's being understood or considered. In fact, there is little understanding at all on either side.

A familiar problem with business ownership is long hours—very long hours. Often, this will come as quite a shock to someone whose only business association was where the males of the family worked regular, predictable, and "normal" hours— that is, nine to five, Monday through Friday, with all weekends, holidays, and vacations free of responsibility. The value system within a family business—as well as the requirements— encourage quite different hours. It is partially these changes in both values and requirements that confuse Elizabeth.

"I believe in hard work," she said. "Nothing worthwhile comes on a silver platter. And, I suppose, to be successful in something as competitive as business, you probably do have to work day and night. But that kind of 'at the top' success doesn't help you be well-rounded or a happy person. I've seen a lot of successful businessmen who are empty as *people* .

"My father-in-law, and probably most business owners, have spent a great part of their lives working and building their businesses. They tend to expect their sons to do the same.

"But, then, most people think they're the best kind of people to be. It's only natural to think other people should be like them, too. This is wrong, because to be really honest, we have to admit that there's room to be many things. My father-in-law likes to think of himself as flexible, so it seems to me if he has any respect for his son at all, he *has* to allow him the freedom to define what's best for himself.

"I don't mean total freedom. I simply mean the ability to have some say as to how he's going to bring his work together with his personal life. If my husband works hard and does his best when he's working, if he enjoys and feels comfortable with what he's doing, then the number of extra hours he spends working shouldn't be part of the yardstick measuring how good a businessman he is.

"If my husband decides that he wants an active, involved family life and uses his time right," she said, "if he meets his commitments, then more shouldn't be asked unless absolutely necessary. Work, on top of work, on top of more work leads to disaster."

Because Elizabeth seems to disassociate herself from the problems of running a family business, she's not aware that circumstances frequently demand extra hours. Elizabeth seems to feel that the extra working hours are a form of discipline rather than a necessary part of making the business successful. She also seems to feel that her father-in-law doesn't really care what she thinks about anything.

"My father-in-law is all wrapped up in his business, and as long as he is, I don't think he ever will really appreciate my needs. Not that he won't try, don't get me wrong, but I think it's just too foreign for him.

"I also think that the family tends to look with wariness and suspicion at me as an interloper. After all, is anybody ever really 'good enough' for their son? His parents sometimes make me feel they think their son could've really done better picking a wife.

"This is really unfair. I don't see where one generation is all that different from any other. The same mistakes are repeated. But instead of the older generation tolerating the younger, they seem to resent being reminded they did the same dumb things, and that feeling tends to widen the gap instead of bridging it.

"My husband and I have made a mutual contract to be a team while we both remain individuals. This is crucial for maintaining my self-respect. But when I express these feelings, his parents almost always read them as a large chip on my shoulder.

"I think a woman must be a person in her own right and have her husband's respect. Then he will unconsciously raise her up in his family's eyes. That way she becomes someone his family must reckon with and they'll allow her her own space."

Elizabeth seems to have forgotten that there have been big changes in thinking in the last 10 years. Women have been given much more opportunity recently to have a say about their life in the business, but her father-in-law was raised in a much more male dominated generation. He probably doesn't even understand what "giving someone their own space" means. Her use of the phrase "reckon with" makes one feel she's looking for a confrontation.

She has a job, too, one of educating his parents to her needs, and not assuming they automatically understand and reject them.

"The fact is that I have the last word every day and there's some power in that. That may not be so important in a marriage of mutual respect like ours, because we *share* our concerns and problems all the time. But when I begin to feel cut out or unappreciated, I know I can can use my power to create dissension.

"I'm a fool if I do, of course, because I could drag my husband down, sap his energy, make him less creative. It's power, yes, but more to do harm than good. The trouble is, his family is making things so uncomfortable for me that sometimes I believe I don't have a lot to lose."

I asked Elizabeth what she felt success meant. Her response was very interesting and important, I think, because it seems to represent the thoughts of so many young women today. Success, she told me, is defining what you need as a person and then being able to fulfil those needs. Part of that, for Elizabeth, is having some influence in some areas of her world.

I've been fortunate to have the chance to meet so many young women like Elizabeth. I enjoy them a great deal, but as I meet more and more families in business, I see more and more often how difficult it is for us sometimes to absorb outsiders who come into our families as "in-laws."

In almost every case, these young women who marry our sons are accepted into our family circle with love, but we don't know soon enough to expect the differences which will arise and how to deal with them. She doesn't share our histories. She doesn't—at least not in the beginning—share our commitments to the business. Her love is for her husband and their life together first. His folks and "their" business just seem to come along as part of the package.

It's very rare—though very welcome—to meet new daughters-in-law who realize marrying a man in a family business means joining in the dreams of all three: the man, the family, and the business.

A workable, loving family relationship with any new family member can't be worked out unless she's willing to cooperate. Her attitude is a key to success. But we have to remember that so much of her attitude depends upon how we accept her during that time she's first getting to know her new family. It depends on *both* of us trying to understand each other's needs, and to respect them, to really see if there is not some way we can all feel good about them.

HOW TO ASSURE HER HELP

I'd like to suggest a few early steps to take to make sure our journey together follows the right path:

1) *Make sure to think always of our son's wife as one of us, not as "her," or "that woman he married."* Our "new daughter" is a full family member. She must be as one of our own children. She will be the mother of our grandchildren. She cannot remain an outsider, even though she comes to us as a stranger.

It's one thing to say that she's part of the family. Many people say that. It's expected. But to *act* as though she is takes a lot of patience, understanding, and energy. Maybe a good way to look at this young woman is as though she were an adopted child. Adoption is a total commitment to the future, and only a total commitment will allow a relationship like this to work.

2) *Make her, from the beginning, a full part of family discussions and planning.* This may be difficult at first. Assuming that we do have family discussions about the future and the business, we

tend to feel much of what we talk about is "private."

A stranger sitting in can really cause a lot of discomfort. But, again, a new daughter-in-law cannot remain a stranger. She's become a member of the family. And the only way we will become comfortable with this new member is to let her know she is accepted.

3) *Discuss the business with her regularly, particularly her husband's place in it.* I don't mean to suggest that we should seek out her advice on business decisions, although in some cases that might be appropriate. What I want to recommend is that she be helped to understand what her husband is working toward, why it takes the time and energy it takes, and—most important—where they fit in our plans for the future. Talk *with*, not *to* her.

We must remember always that Mother and Dad have fashioned their lives. They've built a successful business. Their security is somewhat assured. But successors and their spouses are just beginning to build. Few things are really assured to them, and that often results in much anxiety and fear for them. This is particularly a problem for successors' wives, because their husbands are second only to their fathers-in-law in being lousy communicators.

We can't assume our daughter-in-law understands what we want or expect. We can't assume she understands our confidence—or lack of it—in the future. We can't assume that our gifts will be accepted for the loving gestures they are. Knowledge is power, as wealth is power. If a young woman feels both uninformed and dependent upon others for financial security, she can't help but feel her life is out of her control. Let us always make sure she knows enough to understand our love and good wishes.

4) *Set up some form of objective standard to measure performance and advancement among our successors.* Most business owning couples have more than one child. That implies there will be more than one contender for all roles. But there can only be one chief executive officer—and unless this simple fact is understood, internal warfare is almost inevitable. No specific child of a business owner should ever be allowed to feel "entitled" to become the president. That privilege must be earned.

The above steps may help prevent this problem. At least they will guarantee a receptive audience to our plans. But more than this, we have to set up an environment where confusions, disappointments, and expectations are expressed openly. We must also do what we can to prove to everybody involved that our desire to be "fair" must be translated into making crucial decisions on the basis of what's best for both the family and the business—not for squeaking wheels or family favorites.

Our daughters-in-law deserve much more attention than we normally give them. When they get that attention, we develop the understanding that is crucial to keeping them as our most powerful allies.

CXXXXXXXXXO

Chapter 12

Can't We Declare a Truce?

There are many different ways to look at life in a family business. It's one thing to live that life as a member of the owning-managing family, and an entirely different thing to live it as an outsider, especially as the wife of a potential successor.

Two families we know come to mind. Their stories each represent a side of a common problem people seem to have with "rebellious" daughters-in-law. One is told by a successor, and the other by a successor's wife. I think the experiences and thoughts of these two young people are very representative of a very pervasive complaint.

THE EXHAUSTED SUCCESSOR

I met Jeff at one of our seminars. Late in the week, after we'd had a chance to get to know each other pretty well, he told me over dinner one night that his marriage was close to breaking up. He was very confused.

"I don't know where to turn or what to do," he told me. "This is eating me up inside. I just have to tell someone.

"The whole problem is my Dad—at least I think he's the problem. I don't know. Deborah, my wife, is really depressed about the company and what I'm doing. And she's unbelievably upset about Dad. It's at the point where I think I'm going to have to quit working for him. I can't stand being torn apart like this."

I asked him if his father was aware of the problem he looked up to answer me. His eyes showed his hurt.

"That's the problem," he answered, "Dad's a little bit of a Pollyanna. I mean, he's a sound businessman and everything like that, but in his enthusiasm for what could be, he tends to build things up better than they turn out. He promises things he forgets a week later.

"I believe him. Deb believes him and we make plans and then he changes his mind. For example, I've been working 70 hours a week for what seems like forever. I mentioned to him one day that we wanted to take 10 days and fly to San Francisco. He said fine. Deb was really happy.

"The next day or the day after, we were talking about working and he said how he and I were different from other people, how we loved our work and didn't need vacations.

"I can't explain his effect on me. I just couldn't say anything about the vacation. I felt like to say something would have made me out to be lazy and ungrateful.

"You know, that's the way Dad is. He's a brilliant, talented guy with a personality like a steamroller. You can come to him with a problem and he'll set off on long discussions about life and working and success, and pretty soon your problem has somehow gotten lost. At least, it somehow seems insignificant and selfish.

"He doesn't know he does that. He thinks everything's okay and because he's so strong willed, nobody can tell him when they disagree!"

Jeff seemed to be forgetting that he's made it to adulthood. He's still stuck in the role of "little boy," unable to disagree with his father. This problem will only get worse unless Jeff learns his own strengths and becomes able to gently, but firmly remind Dad of agreements they've made. After all, as Jeff said, his Dad forgets. He's not trying to mess up their lives.

We knew Jeff's father, and we knew what he was going to have to face if Jeff left the business. He'd assumed the business would go to Jeff, his only child. Jeff's Dad was 66 and there was hardly enough time to find and train another successor to the $3-4 million business. Jeff's departure would be a tragedy for the business and for the family.

The problem with the cancelled vacation was only one of many problems.

"It happens over and over again," Jeff complained. "How is Deb going to understand why Dad would rather see me play golf with customers than spend time with her and our children? How can I tell him I have money problems *now*, when he plans on giving me the business someday?

"Oh, it's a whole range of things, and Deb's telling me she can't stand it anymore. She doesn't think Dad respects her because she's a woman. She's given up trying to talk to him because she believes he doesn't really listen. And, because he changes his story so often, she thinks he exaggerates the potentials of the business. That scares her, too."

Jeff made it seem as though his Dad wanted him to neglect his wife and son to give preference to customers, but I'd be willing to bet he was misreading his father's motives. How could he find out, though, other than by explaining Deb's interpretation so that his Dad could see the potential problems and work out a better solution with his son?

"Deb's scared and telling me she wants out. She's so emotional about it, I can't really talk to her anymore. I know if I don't leave, I'll lose Deb. But I know if I do leave, I'll kill Dad."

Again, I have to repeat the importance of communication. Jeff is as much a part of the problem as his father because (a) he doesn't remind his Dad of his promises and plans, and (b) he's obviously not talking to his wife to keep her up to date on events as they happen. He seems to hope that maybe problems will go away if he ignores them. His lack of action is surely contributing to the tension that's resulted.

Why does Deb feel the way she does? What's happening to her to bring her to the point of forcing her husband to give up something as important to him as his family's business? One way to understand can be to look at the problem through the eyes of someone like Deb.

THE AGGRESSIVE DAUGHTER-IN-LAW

Sylvia is a daughter-in-law from a different family. She doesn't know Deb. They've never met. Yet I have a feeling that they'd understand each other very well if they did.

When I first met Sylvia, she was very bitter, bitter enough to begin telling me about her situation almost as soon as she heard that we worked with family businesses. To summarize her opinion, she felt she'd been unjustly treated by her in-laws.

"Richard's folks have been critical of me since the first time we ever had a real conversation," she said, "and their judgments have always been negative."

Sylvia explained that she was the daughter-in-law of a business owner, and the wife of his probable successor. The family was having problems. Although the father and son worked well together, the two couples seemed to set off sparks in each other's presence.

"We're such totally different people," she said. "While I think I'm able to understand and accept the way Morrie and Susan are, they always seem to want me to be like *them* ."

I asked her to give me an example.

"Well," she answered, "about six months ago, we got together, the four of us, to talk this through once and for all. It was a good talk—and one of the decisions was that we had to be more open with each other, and I agreed.

"About two months later, Richard and I had lunch with his father and I got a lot of things off my chest. I tend to say what I think, probably too much, but I try to be honest. People always know what's on my mind.

"Anyway, I think Richard's been doing too many things that aren't directly helping him get more stature in the company. His salary depends on his earning power, but Richard's earning power is being held up while he 'learns.' I don't think this is a good situation and that's what I told Morrie.

"But my father-in-law just got more and more upset with me. I could see he was getting upset, but I was acting on our decision to be more open, so I went ahead and said what I thought.

"By the end of that talk, he made it very obvious that he wanted me out of his sight. I got on his nerves.

"He doesn't like to be disagreed with, in general, and I guess I make it worse by being so...so *aggressive* . I try to be tactful, but my back gets up and I say too much, too bluntly. The result, as I see it, is that Richard is going to suffer because of my personality."

I asked Sylvia to tell me why she thought Richard was getting such a bad deal from his father, and she immediately explained that she didn't think it was a bad deal, exactly. Explaining what she really meant seemed to cause her some problem, though.

"We have our own way of life, Katy," she said. "When Richard worked for Standard Steel (*not the company's real name*) and I was teaching, we managed to build a good life. It was hard, but we made good money and got used to living very comfortably.

"Then Morrie talked Richard into joining the business. Morrie being Morrie, he really built it up and Richard was hooked. It really looked like a super opportunity.

"So Richard quit his job, I quit teaching, and we moved. In anticipation of all these great things, we bought a bigger house with a bigger mortgage. We were willing to take an effective cut in income, but only because we thought it would be a very temporary situation.

"I didn't know Morrie very well then, so I wasn't used to his enthusiasm and exaggeration. Richard knew, I guess, but he believed in the pie in the sky, too.

"That was three years ago. Since then our daughter was born. Richard's salary has barely increased 10% a year. With inflation, that means our real income is dropping every year.

"But Richard's family look at the things we built up while both of us were working and think we've got it made—far beyond what we should, at our age anyway. I think they think we throw money away.

"Well, we're eating into our savings, and I'm getting scared. It's not just the money, either. Richard's morale and feelings of self-worth are involved.

"He joined his father to do the things he's good at, as well as to learn. But there never seems to be any time to invest in his ideas or talents."

Sylvia was so upset that she began to blush.

"I'm so confused," she said. "I'm scared that I'm driving a wedge between Richard and his father. I'm scared that we're financially in over our heads. I don't know what we'll do if things don't work out...Richard's not building any useable skills, and, with the baby, I'm not able to teach any more.

"And I have to tell you it hurts me to feel that Morrie and Susan don't like me. They're nice people, but they always pass judgments. They think what they think, and have no room to understand how helpless I feel.

"They just think I'm aggressive and greedy, and what they think is what they *know* is right.

"But I want it to work. Richard loves the business, and there seems to be a good future in it...but that future depends on how I get along with two people who don't seem to like me, two people who now don't seem to want to bother to understand.

"The last time we got together, Morrie and Susan spent the night in small talk, as though the problem didn't exist. But I can't ignore something that's eating away at me, so I wound up ruining everybody's time, mine included."

A daughter-in-law is probably one of the more volatile members of the business owner's "instant family," not only because of her love and concern for her successor/husband, but also because she comes from an entirely different family. She starts off as a stranger, so she usually doesn't understand her new in-laws any more than they understand her.

I've learned that when two people have a problem and they get a third person in the middle, there's rarely a solution, only bad feelings. Sylvia believes she has spoken up for her husband. She's believes she has expressed her concern about family matters surrounding her husband. The trouble is that this behavior is not very constructive.

Because there's lack of understanding among these four people—each one is only thinking of his own hurt—they are making judgments about each other based on emotion rather than fact.

It's not Sylvia's battle with the in-laws. She didn't make any conditions; and, since almost everything came through her husband, she has little direct knowledge of what the agreements were. It would be one thing if she could say "when we sat down, Dad, you said X, but now you're saying Y...," but she can't, because he really didn't talk to her. He should have, of course, but since he didn't, she's forced to depend on hearsay and subjective interpretations of her husband's comments.

Unlike Sylvia, I had a chance to talk with her father-in-law. It was a few weeks later at a dinner party. We had talked for a while and Sylvia naturally came up in the conversation. Like Sylvia, Morrie felt a compulsion to talk.

"I don't know what to do with that girl," he said. "She seems convinced I'm out to hang Richard by his thumbs or something.

"She wants everything at once. She thinks Richard's unappreciated and exploited, when, if anything, he's overpaid. I mean, I don't begrudge him the money, but he's got a long way to go before he's really effective. All the cash flow is generated by me. He's being paid for potential, and generously, as far as I'm concerned.

"This business is now supporting two families, where it used to support only one, and I feel that my keeping this company together for Richard's future is the important thing. Money comes later.

"Susan and I had it tough in the early years, and no young woman is going to come crying to me about how tough her life is. At their age, we were living on franks and beans—when we had them. Nobody's going to lecture me about hard times.

"As for his being overworked, I'm the one who's always on the road. Sure, he works hard, but not as hard as I do. I just don't accept that.

"As far as we're concerned, we've done all we can. The ball is now in their court."

IS IT ANYBODY'S FAULT?

Was Morrie saying he'd suffered, therefore she, too, had to suffer? Was he forgetting that two different generations come with two different sets of assumptions?

Morrie may have had in the back of his mind the idea that he'd deliberately make it tough for his son, but, if so, this should have been made clear. He hadn't told Richard that he wanted him to work hard, to come up through the ranks, to experience some of what he experienced. Morrie should have told Richard that hurting now would lead to some good rewards tomorrow. That's fine, provided it's made explicit—and that Richard explicitly agrees.

Sylvia labled herself "aggressive," and stated that she's been outlawed—partially because of her attitude, but also because of the position Morrie put them into. Her point that she shouldn't be cast into a role seems valid, because families have a way of defining their own reality, and if someone is defined as "aggressive," they are then, in fact, aggressive, even though they may be the most timid person in the world.

Sylvia's by no means blameless. She seems to be getting involved where she shouldn't be, when what's really needed is for Richard to learn to open his mouth. He has to be brought back into contact with his father. Instead, what Sylvia's doing is trying to fill the vacuum left by her "silent" husband. She may be aggressive, but a lot of that is because she's being forced into a job that should belong to her husband.

Morrie, on his part, is overplaying his hardship a little, but Sylvia is probably as much a martyr as her father-in-law. Poor us, she is saying, we're in this expensive house, in this expensive neighborhood. We gave this up. We gave that up. Without arguing the point of whether or not their life was "ruined," it seems safe to comment that everyone is responsible for his or her *own* life.

Each of us is responsible for making decisions, choices, and changes. To say someone else forced us into our situation, that we're stuck with it, really doesn't make a lot of sense. If we don't accept it, there are usually many ways to get out.

THE HAPLESS GORILLA'S WIFE

I don't want to ignore another very common—and difficult—situation, that of the daughter married to a son-in-law successor. There is a great deal of difference between a son and a son-in-law in a family-owned business, and a woman married to a non-family successor faces some very real obstacles.

For example, what will a business owner's daughter think or do when her brother(s) are advanced ahead of her husband, in spite of what she sees as her husband's "superior" talents? How do we define the difference between the rights by blood and the rights by merit? Who is to decide?

My husband has said that sons-in-law tend to remain vice presidents, no matter what their capabilities, because Dad resents the "gorilla" who's sleeping with his baby. There's some truth to this exaggeration, but, of course, there's more to it than this. A son-in-law is *not* blood. He comes from the outside. He has different thoughts and tastes. He's hard to fit into the family.

Someday an entire book will be written on this subject alone. For now, I would like to suggest that every family work very hard to treat each new member—daughter-in-law or son-in-law—as though he or she were "real" family. The fact is, they *are* members of the family. They are treated as something else only at our peril and the peril of the business.

People are people. Think about Sylvia or Deborah. Think about our daughters whose husbands want to work with us. I think it's important for us to try to understand them a little better, while we think about what we will have to do to help them understand us.

~~~~~~~~~~~~

Getting on and Getting Better

Chapter 13

Who Wants To Retire?

Twenty years ago, a couple I know—Alan and Adelle—started a business in their basement. That business now does more than $3 million in sales from a new plant in an industrial park.

Through the years, Adelle stayed very involved in the business, even though she was raising two sons. Today she is the treasurer and works half days, 5 days a week.

But Adelle has a problem, a very difficult problem.

Three years ago, Alan, Sr. had a serious heart attack. Their two sons, Alan, 31, and Dick, 28, rose to fill the gap. For the three months it took for their father to recover, they ran the business together.

This situation would ordinarily sound ideal, but a conflict has come up, one that's not easy to solve.

Last year, Alan, Sr. had open heart surgery, and, although he's still a relatively young man at 59, he's been persuaded by his doctor that he should retire.

Adelle loves her husband and wants to enjoy retirement with him, but she, herself, is not ready to give up working in the company.

Adelle has given more than 20 years to the business, and it's been a focal point of her life. At 54, she's vital and energetic and feels a need to stay involved with the business, both for herself and to help guide her sons.

In many ways Adelle's facing the same sort of problem Alan and other entrepreneurs face when the question of retirement comes up. But her husband's forced retirement adds a new dimension to the problem.

Good estate planning contemplates the implications of the sequential death of the marriage partners. Similarly, if the death or retirement of the male business head creates the role of the "working wife in charge" of a family business, then the question of *her* retirement takes on an entirely new dimension—and must be considered.

If the business is to continue, the development of successor management becomes vital, and yet it's often at odds with mother's needs and matriarchal management.

Adelle has come full circle working with her husband, and is now facing a demand that she retire. Like the committed owner-manager, Adelle hasn't had the chance or the need to get involved in the sorts of outside activities and interests that now could keep her happy, active, and productive in "retirement."

She learned, too, the importance of sharing her problems. For a while, she faced it alone and kept her feelings and concerns to herself. But as Alan's recuperation from his heart attack progressed and their retirement plans became a more and more frequent topic, Adelle recognized how much this man she loved, and the life they shared, would be affected by her decision. In fact, she realized the decision was going to have to be theirs, not only hers.

They talked about and reached a kind of compromise, to sort of ease into Alan's retirement. Adelle would continue to work for the time being—half days as she always had. But there would be two major exceptions.

First, they would spend the afternoons exploring what they labeled "the dubious gift of leisure." They've always worked well together, now they have to find out how well they can play together. Secondly, for the first time in 20 years they are going to take vacations of more than 3 days in duration.

She and her husband are now ready to reap the considerable harvest that has come from their work together.

Where else but in a family business could a husband and wife have the opportunity to build their legacy together?

SUFFERING FROM RETIREMENT

"Dad's been retired for 18 months now, and he reminds me of a derailed train. It breaks my heart to watch him. His wheels are still turning, his boilers are fired up, but he's got no track to run on..."

This young man was talking about his father, an active man who started his company at age 32. It began as a small operation in California, and in the following 36 years grew into a county-wide distributorship grossing almost $15 million in sales.

But this founder retired relatively suddenly, with very little preparation. He got fed up one day with what he felt was the increasing harassment of an excessively welfare government, and just walked out. He called his son and said, "Here, you fight it."

"Dad's always been a dedicated golfer," his son, Louis, told me, "but somehow, when he retired he became an obsessed golfer. I mean, he throws himself into the game, plays mean and hard, and by the time he comes off the course, he's really miserable. It's not fun for him anymore.

"It's hard to believe, but I'd say he hates the game now."

Louis's father is suffering from retirement, and I'm sure this means his mother is suffering from retirement, also.

Another woman, Janet, suffers from retirement too. Her husband also stopped working less than a year ago, leaving his machine tool company to his three sons.

"We disagree a lot more about things now," she told me. "We never really used to, at least not very much, mainly because Bill never was much of a talker. He'd always hurry through meals, spend a lot of time at the office. You know, we wouldn't have a chance to quarrel.

"But now I don't know what it is, but he's edgy. He's always picking on things and criticizing. We have argument after argument. I think he just has too much time on his hands."

DOES IT HAVE TO BE?

Experiences like these aren't unusual. Business owners often retire unprepared for a totally different existence. They work for years in a world requiring aggressiveness, a world full of pressure and tension. They have tremendous psychological momentum and when the load is removed, usually suddenly, they and their concerned families face new problems.

As a retired beer distributor once told me:

"You know, I learned too late that I should have *planned* on getting out of the business someday, and realized that both my environment and life style were going to change," he said. "After I sold the business, it seemed like I was doing everything wrong. I was at home a lot more then and Dorothy and I, we'd go at it like cats and dogs.

"I never was around her so much before. And as far as golf goes, I got so miserable on the fairway that nobody wanted to go out with me anymore.

"Finally I figured out that I missed all the problems in the business. I loved them—the sales, getting deliveries out and in on time, even having a few beers with tavern owners. I used to go from six in the morning to, sometimes, nine or ten at night, driving trucks, throwing cases around with the drivers, juggling invoices.

"When I sold out, that was suddenly all over. But I felt healthy, strong as hell. Still do. I wanted to keep working, but the brewery really put a lot of pressure on me to retire. Thank God and Dorothy, that I came to my senses and got involved in some worthwhile things."

This founder is now on a hospital board, heads the local United Fund drive, and even does a little consulting with other distributors through his association. His outlook has improved so much that even his sons now call him in for advice. He loves it.

Too bad all retirements don't work out as well.

A WIFE'S ROLE

If you and your husband are in your 40's, it's not too late. If you are in your 50's, you'd better hustle. If you have reached the 60's, you'd better start yesterday.

To do what? To start thinking about retirement.

Because I'm writing to wives of *successful* business owners, I'm going to assume that the financial side of retirement—our security in the coming years—has been planned out and isn't a problem. I know that's assuming a lot, but let's just set financial considerations aside for now.

Successful retirement is so much more than having enough money. It's a blending of our ideas and dreams for the future with our husbands' plans and needs. And that's a complicated task.

The nature of the beast we live with is that he probably is a "workalovics," and I think we have to accept the fact that this probably won't change. The trouble is that *he* often doesn't realize he won't be able to change.

Our husbands may think that it will be just great to play golf whenever they want to, or to sit in the sun and let somebody else do the work. That may even be true, in the short run. But over the long haul, they're going to remain "workalovics." Golf and hammocks are going to wear pretty thin, pretty fast.

We, on the other hand, probably won't have our husbands' problems. We may be involved in charity, or in political and community projects. We may have many interests, including the households we manage. But our husbands have been so busy building and running their businesses, they probably haven't had either the interest, the time or the energy to get involved in worthwhile outside activities.

This is why retirement planning is so important, and it's an area where we, as wives, must help.

Everyone needs a reason to get up in the morning. We can't just put in time sitting on rocking chairs watching the snow fall, because if either one of us is unhappy, that means a doubly unhappy couple. *Our husbands must retire from something to something* .

Remember that we've developed different lifestyles during the times we've been apart—the "working" hours. When he retires from his job, his life will change very drastically. And ours will have to adjust too. These adjustments can't be made overnight.

There's a fine old proverb I reflect on often which says, *"For the ignorant, old age is as winter; for the learned, it is a harvest."*

It implies so much. Winter is something that just happens to people, while a harvest is an active, joyful process—a reward for the planning and effort that went before.

Retirement can bring with it a priceless gift—the hours and days we will have available to spend together. We should be planning ways to keep our husbands healthy, interested, and productive in their "harvest" years. What we want to achieve is a retirement so fulfilling and successful that we will eventually see it as a new beginning, a renaissance, rather than the rejection it is so often considered to be.

HEALTH IS AN INVESTMENT

In looking ahead to retirement, one of the first jobs we, as wives of business owners, have to tackle is to convince our husbands to take care of their health. Nothing will ruin a well-planned, successful future faster than poor health.

Most business owners take better care of their cars than they do of their bodies. Their hectic world creates an almost inevitable drain on the resources of their bodies and since they're not likely to change on their own, it's up to us to take the initiative.

It's a major project. I know from experience. There's just no easy way to convince Ol' Dad directly that he should pay attention to good nutrition and learn to enjoy some type of exercise. Instead, what seems to work best is to work so skillfully and painlessly that he hardly notices that we're changing his bad habits.

What he should notice is how much better he feels, not how we're going about changing his habits.

The first major objective should probably be exercise. My own husband, for example, doesn't care for tennis, golf or other social sports. He does enjoy puttering around in the garden and mowing the lawn, but since we have only a small flower garden and a riding mower for the grass, that's not really exercise. He says he loves to walk, but when he does, he mostly stands around and enjoys the scenery.

Walking has a real potential. It's something that can be done together. It can be done anytime in almost any place.

Brisk walking increases our need for oxygen. It makes the lungs and heart work harder, and as they work harder, circulation increases. This in turn stretches veins and arteries, making them more flexible.

The body is a remarkable machine. It responds to exercise, no matter what its age.

The question, of course, is how to get our husbands to walk. I'm working on it with mine, but it's not easy. Maybe the answer to my problem is a Great Dane puppy who demands a brisk stroll every day—becoming more demanding and "brisker" as he grows.

Diet is another important health consideration. Add too many fatty foods and excess weight to lack of exercise and you come up with the potential for a whole string of medical problems.

I know some women who've taken cooking classes to learn to make meals with fewer calories and less fat. They say they've found recipes that are so good that their husbands don't feel deprived of the special foods they enjoy.

And "reducing" diets can be flexible. If we like a quiet cocktail before dinner or a glass of wine with our meals, we needn't give them up. A little knowledge of nutrition will show how to write them into a reducing diet. The ultimate objective, of course, is to develop new eating habits.

The major lesson most owner-managers' wives learn after their husbands retire is that it seems to fall on Mom's shoulders to keep Dad on the straight and narrow. Our husbands have worked so hard and sacrificed so much for so long that the very idea of self-discipline has got to be the farthest thing from their minds.

The habits of regular exercise, good eating, and self-discipline have to be acquired long before retirement if we're going to enjoy our long-deserved harvest years together.

LET'S NOT OVERDO IT

But retirement isn't so simple as just assuring good health. In fact, the *concern* about health can often become as disabling as the heart attack or stroke. I'm reminded most vividly of one family I met a few years back in which both the founder and the successor had suffered heart attacks.

I remember sitting with Lou, the successor, and his wife, Lynn, on the first backyard glider I'd seen in years. We were working together on a benefit concert, but the conversation eventually drifted around to the subject of Lou's father.

"The situation is getting just unbearable," Lou told me. "Since his heart attack, Dad's turned into some kind of guru. He sits around all day doing deep breathing or yoga or reading books on transcendental meditation. He won't talk to anybody—at least not about the business.

"He's unwinding, he says. Slowing down. We all should, he says.

"Well, for a lot of people that's true, but there's a substantial business here to run and Dad's not running it anymore and he's not letting any of us take over.

"I've put 15 years into this thing and now it's my life. If it goes *splutt*, I don't know what I ... we're going to be able to do!"

Lynn's face had reddened slightly and she was looking at Lou with concern.

"I just *hate* what this whole thing is doing to Lou, Katy," she said. "His father is driving Lou up a wall and I don't know if I'll ever forgive him for that.

"Sometimes I think Dad's lost his marbles since the heart attack. We try to talk to Mom but all she does is side with him and send us books on 'Type A' personalities."

It happened that Léon and I had dinner with Lou's father and mother, Ben and Carole, a few weeks later. We spent most of our time talking about health and how the pace of modern life was unnatural. Lou's father even used his son as an example.

"Lou does okay, you know," he said, "but he works too hard. Did you know he's had a heart attack too? Thirty-eight and he's driving himself into the ground. I tell him but he won't listen."

Ben explained how he even kept Lou's salary down to try to get him to work less hard.

"I see him killing himelf just like I did. I tell him he's got to change—I give him books, I try to talk to him. He won't listen. I'm not going to encourage the way he's acting. No way."

After an embarrassed silence, the subject was changed. Later, Carole and I went to the powder room.

"How do Ben and Lou get along, Carole?" I asked once we were alone.

"You can see!" she answered. "They don't. I love both of them, Katy and I'm stuck square in the middle. They don't talk to each other. They don't talk to me ... and I don't know what's going to happen to the business."

"Could Lou run the business, Carole?"

"I think so," she answered without looking up. "He has to. If something happens to Ben—with his heart—Lou is the only hope for the business..."

"But?"

"But Ben is right. Our son is working himself into a grave. If he doesn't slow down, I'm afraid of what will happen. What good will the business be then?"

"Carole," I asked, "Lou said that your husband isn't really running the business anymore. Is that true?"

"I think so," she said, after a pause. "Something has snapped inside him when he had the heart attack. He was always a quiet man, worked like a stevedore. But now ... I don't know. He's stopped working hard and this relaxation thing is becoming a religion with him.

"I can't tell him, either. I mean, I love Ben, of course. We've had some wonderful years. But I don't agree with what he's doing to Lou. We have so much money—more than we need—but Ben feels that money would destroy Lou, that it's our last hold over him.

"Please try to get Ben to listen, Katy." she said. "He's got to listen before it's too late."

I said we would try, but I guessed, even then, that whatever solution we came to, Carole would have to supply the keystone. The two men, by themselves, were sliding deeper and deeper into a hole. They didn't realize what was truely important about planning for retirement.

IT ALL TAKES PLANNING

Remember that retirement *can* be a renaissance. Retirement is nothing short of a new career, a move into new challenges, reaping the benefit of a lot of hard-won victories. Yet most business owners either avoid the subject totally, or else they assume that it will all work out somehow, once it happens.

A very good friend of ours knew that retirement wouldn't just "work out" all by itself. He planned for his and now claims he's having more fun than when he actually ran the business.

"I planned my retirement for almost five years in advance," he explains proudly whenever the question is asked. "You know what I'm doing now? My daughter runs the restaurant completely—with all the headaches and the fun—and I'm doing what I always loved.

"I personally make the house salads, the ones we became famous for. I've worked out a real performance for the tables, and I meet most of the customers personally. I love it. I'm pretty sure the customers love it, too. You know, I think I'm becoming to our restaurant what Colonel Sanders was to his fried chicken."

Jack stays out of the day to day operation, trying as hard as he can not to be one of those retirees who mess up the business part time. Mostly, he succeeds.

As he puts it: "I just help out when my daughter asks me, and I give the place some *class* ."

And "class" is something Jack's retirement gives to him. I only wish I could see it happen more often. Every business man deserves it.

CRRRRRRRRR

Postscript

They Should Give Us a Medal

Many people, watching us from the outside, think we have it made.

We often hear about our "nice" life, our "easy" life, from our friends and our neighbors. We hear this, and although it's difficult, we soon learn to rely on our sense of humor to help us keep our sharp responses to ourselves.

In fact, if we didn't spend a lot of time trying to laugh, I'm afraid we'd have to spend even more time crying.

This book has only touched the surface of a very large and important subject. Business ownership is not just a man's game. It's not even *mainly* a man's game. In fact, I think we should stop thinking of it as a game altogether.

Building and running a successful family business is a serious, rewarding, and valuable occupation. We are building—together, as a family—opportunity and privilege future generations would not have otherwise.

We aren't beneficiaries of somebody else's hard work. We are partners in that hard work. That's a little easier to accept for those of us who are actively involved in the business, but for those of us who don't sell, or juggle accounts, or manage manufacturing plants there is work and worry and struggle just the same.

Whatever form our involvement takes, we women who inhabit the fascinating, troublesome world of the successful family business, have struggled fiercely and bravely for every benefit we enjoy.

If we are founder's wives, we have to learn very early how to cope with the loneliness of the 14-hour workday, the frustration of managing finances when there just isn't enough money to pay all the bills. On top of that job, we have to try to convince our children that owning our own business is the best way of life in the world.

If we are successors' wives, we have to learn quickly to swallow our fears and frustrations in the knowledge and hope that the bright future we're working towards will come to be. We have to know how and when to support our spouses, and we have to know when to be more demanding of our own rights to understand and control our destinies—and when to wait a little longer.

If we are wives of successful business owners, we have, somehow, to find the compassion, courage, and humor to be the buffer between our children, working in the business, and their father. We have to see that our "in-law" children are not kept as out-laws by us or by other members of our family.

We all have to help our husbands learn that someday they must let go. We have to make sure they prepare for this. We must help them understand how to give up the power without feeling that everything worthwhile in life has ended. And while we're teaching all this, we have to learn it ourselves.

We all have to make sure the chosen successors are patient and not threatening to their father. We have to learn to mediate, to balance immediate needs against future requirements. We have to keep our family together.

We all will have, somehow, to find the courage to face the statistical fact that we will probably someday be widows. We have to find the courage to get involved with our estate planning. We have to force ourselves to be prepared for whatever the future has in store.

We do the very best we can. Events won't always turn out the way we want them to, but we can—we must—learn to accept what we can't change.

We can be proud that we've provided the love and understanding, the commitment and compassion, that helped make—and keep—our family company successful. We should be proud that we are the women who, with our men, build and run successful family businesses.

I hope that in some small way, this book has helped the rest of the world become a little proud of us, too.

CXXXXXXXXXX